Fund Your Future

Winning Strategies for Managing Your Mutual Funds and 401(k)

Julie Stav

with Lisa Rojany-Buccieri

B

BERKLEY BOOKS, NEW YORK

B

A Berkley Book
Published by The Berkley Publishing Group
A division of Penguin Group (USA) Inc.
375 Hudson Street
New York, New York 10014

This publication is designed to provide accurate and authoritative information in regard to the subject matter covered. It is sold with the understanding that the publisher is not engaged in rendering legal, accounting, or other professional services. If you require legal advice or other expert assistance, you should seek the services of a competent professional.

Copyright © 2001, 2004 by Julie Stav.
Cover author photograph copyright © by Charles William Bush Photography.
Cover design by Lesley Worrell.
Text design by Tiffany Kukec.

All rights reserved.
This book, or parts thereof, may not be reproduced in any form without permission.
The scanning, uploading, and distribution of this book via the Internet or via any other means without the permission of the publisher is illegal and punishable by law. Please purchase only authorized electronic editions, and do not participate in or encourage electronic piracy of copyrighted materials. Your support of the author's rights is appreciated.
BERKLEY and the "B" design are trademarks belonging to Penguin Group (USA) Inc.

PRINTING HISTORY
Berkley hardcover edition / December 2001
Berkley trade paperback edition / June 2004

Berkley trade paperback ISBN: 0-425-19605-4

The Library of Congress has cataloged the Berkley hardcover edition as follows:

Stav, Julie.
Fund your future : winning strategies for managing your mutual funds and 401(k) /
Julie Stav with Lisa Rojany-Buccieri.
p. cm.
ISBN 0-425-18361-0
1. Mutual funds. 2. 401(k) plans. I. Rojany-Buccieri, Lisa. II. Title.
HG4530. S78 2001
332.024'01—dc21   2001043572

PRINTED IN THE UNITED STATES OF AMERICA

10 9 8 7 6 5 4 3 2 1

Most Berkley Books are available at special quantity discounts for bulk purchases for sales promotions, premiums, fund-raising, or educational use. Special books, or book excerpts, can also be created to fit specific needs.

For details, write: Special Markets, The Berkley Publishing Group, 375 Hudson Street, New York, New York 10014.

To Danny, Tony, and Jonathan, my most precious assets.
—JS

To Kristian, Olivia, and Chloe, the loves of my life.
—LRB

ACKNOWLEDGMENTS

To Lisa, who lovingly added this book to her nursing schedule. Your good sense of humor kept me laughing and your discipline kept me on track. To Val, thank you for being so supportive and filling in whenever needed. I appreciate your unselfish help. To Diane, thank you for keeping my feet on the ground but letting my head fly with the wind. To Denise, I have a tremendous respect for the quality of your work and the greatness of your heart. To Danny, the wind beneath my wings, thank you for being my biggest fan. Thank you all.

—JS

Thanks are due to so many people who rallied behind me when the arrival of our newborn twins ran smack-dab into the book schedule, including Kristian, who is the best new daddy ever; our parents and family who shower my daughters with love; and Julie, who didn't mind the slurping noises in the background. Thanks also to Chuck Hurewitz for introducing me to Julie— finally, a soulmate who understands math and has taught me so much about life, not to mention finances.

—LRB

CONTENTS

Have you ever thought about your financial goals and how much money you would need to accomplish your dreams? What are those dreams, anyway? Is it to send your children to college, to buy a house, to help your parents financially, to be able to stop working for a living?

Are you putting away enough money for the future? How is your 401(k) performing? How do you choose among the investment choices you are given? Is it better to buy individual stocks or mutual funds? Or should you invest in an IRA or in a two-year CD? And by the way, what the heck is an IRA or a mutual fund, anyway? Confusing? You bet!

I used to think about my financial future and get so overwhelmed that I would end up fantasizing that I won the lottery. With the jackpot in mind, I would let my mind drift, and I would list the many ways that I would spend the money: a new house, a trip around the world, a shoe collection that would make Imelda Marcos jealous. I'd bargain with my fairy godmother, promising to donate half my winnings to her favorite charity if she would just be so kind as to give me that lottery. Then, when the inevitable happened and some other (clearly less worthy) soul got the winning ticket, I would be back to where I started, wondering how in the heck I was going to manage to fund my future. Can you relate?

What's the difference between people with no money worries and you? What's the difference between you and people who can afford to send their kids to college, pay for their lavish weddings, and still live out their own retirement dreams?

Okay, maybe some of them inherited millions from Great-Grandpa Moneypenny, but the majority were probably once like you. They worked hard for their money, too, putting in all the hours, attending all the meetings, dealing with all the crazy demands, and working all those weekends. And they also probably walked around with that nagging little voice in their head questioning the stability of their financial future.

The real difference between them and you is only this: They set financial goals and committed themselves to an investment course that would enable them to reach those goals. Bottom line: They took control of their financial future. And you can, too. You don't need to hire some expensive, big-shot financial planner. The truth is, *there is no one who has as much vested in the outcome of your financial planning as you do*. So it makes sense that you should be in control of your money. Who else knows what is important to you, how much money you need, and how much risk you're willing to take to reach your goals?

If you're like a lot of people who blindly follow the recommendations of a financial advisor or flashy money guru without taking the time to learn the basics and keep abreast of your investment choices, at some point or another, you're bound to find yourself up the proverbial creek, paddling madly to get a grasp on your finances. But as long as you have taken the time to learn where you want to go with your money, you should have no trouble funding your future and living out your dreams. It's simply a matter of evaluating your personal circumstances, figuring out your goals, assessing your investment temperament, and choosing the right investment options.

After that scary-sounding list of to-dos, some of you might be getting a little intimidated right about now. Numbers were never your "thing," and the thought of burying yourself in a sea of numbers or investment terms feels as exciting as a visit to the dentist. Why can't these experts just speak English? Why can't they lighten up with all those secret agent spy codes—401(k), 403(b), W-4, IRA? Why does it have to be so confusing?

I used to be intimidated by financial and stock market lingo, too. Fancy terms and big numbers made my head spin. Following the unwritten rule that "girls are good with words, boys are good with numbers," I took pride in my flowery essays while my brother got As in algebra. Well, guess what?

Money is green; it's neither blue nor pink.

When I really buckled down and tackled the stock market and mutual funds, I realized that we really don't have much use for all those fancy terms and numbers anyway. A calculator, a magnifying glass (why they make those numbers so small is probably part of the plot to intimidate us), and a solid determination to turn gibberish into serious cash is all we need to begin to see our money multiply, even while we sleep. Talk about being financially powerful!

In my first book, *Get Your Share*, I tried to educate and motivate anyone who wished to participate in the stock market but who didn't know where to begin. We started with the very basic principles of what a stock is and why and how a company issues shares in order to raise money to expand its business. Through humor, analogies, and just plain talk, we studied the state of the market in general to determine the most advantageous moment to invest in a stock. We looked for a hot sector, a hot industry, and the hottest companies within that industry that potentially have what it takes to be the biggest and most profitable companies of tomorrow.

We were like race car drivers: We knew where we wanted to go and made sure we had high-performance individual stocks to get us there. We looked under the hood to confirm that our car had the horsepower to outperform the tough competition. We made sure all systems were go, and when the time was right, we stepped on the gas at full throttle, fueled by the anticipation of success and the thrill of the race. Sure, there was some risk involved, but that was part of the excitement—and the potential gains made it all worth it.

But some of us don't want to be race car drivers, especially when the track suddenly veers off a cliff. It's a lot of work to stay on the road. You must always be ready for the unexpected. Decisions need to be made quickly, and if you make a mistake, you can get hurt—as anyone who spun out of control in the high-tech crash of 2000 will recall. High performance comes with high maintenance.

Car racing is not for the faint of heart and neither is playing the stock market. It takes discipline and hard work to choose the best stock, buy at the right time, and know when to cut losses or cash in profits.

Many investors enjoy the daily work and get a rush watching their stocks perform. And the stock market is not just for the affluent or high-powered money brokers. Nor do you need a degree in economics. In *Get Your Share*, I showed readers that we all can benefit from the stock market—even so far as to invest on-line with no minimum outlay. With as little as twenty dollars, we can open a brokerage account and begin trading, applying the same sound principles the bigwigs in fancy offices and designer suits use with billions of dollars. Or we can form investment clubs, where fun and finance mix as well as chocolate and peanut butter.

But I know that many of you still feel left out in the cold. You wish you could have access to the potential gains that individual stock ownership can provide, but careers, family commitments, busy lifestyles, aversion to risk, or perhaps just lack of interest have kept you from getting involved in the stock market. You want to go places, but you don't want the high-speed race.

Well, let me put your mind at ease. In *Fund Your Future*, I will show you how you can arrive, refreshed and relaxed, at your financial destination by letting others do the driving for you in a car built for comfort, endurance, and fuel efficiency. I will show you how to profit by investing in the stock market through the use of mutual funds. Mutual funds constitute a powerful basket of money collected from regular people like us and invested by the mutual fund company, which then buys and sells individual stocks on our behalf. With mutual funds, we get to be the passengers. Mutual fund managers do what we don't want to do. They watch our money on a daily basis and make the necessary adjustments to our accounts to stay on course. We just need to know how to pick the mutual fund that is going our way, taking the route we want to take, and going at the speed we want to go.

And speaking of choices, many employers offer 401(k) plans. A 401(k) is a company-sponsored, pretax retirement plan. Lots of us have access to incredible returns through mutual funds in the retirement programs our employers offer, and yet we don't have a clue as to how to profit from them. In this book, I am going to teach you how to work that money hard by making the right choices within your 401(k) plan as well.

But before we fasten our seat belts, we have to take a look at your starting point. We have to evaluate your current financial position in order to chart the best course. After all, there are several lanes on the road to success. Then we need to make sure we know what your destination is, so we can set specific financial goals. Whether you are planning for retirement, looking to buy a new home, seeking to resolve credit card debt, or starting a college fund for your kids, we need to determine how much money you are going to need.

Once we know where you are going, using your time frame and tolerance for risk as the starting point, I will help you make the best investment choices. If you don't know a stock from a bond and get baffled when you try to balance your checkbook, don't worry. What I'm about to teach you is not complicated. And it is never too late to learn.

I used to be like many of you. I thought I could largely ignore my financial situation until tomorrow, or next weekend, or whenever I could manage to sit down and figure it all out. But then I drove into a pothole. The pothole came in the form of a divorce that left me a single mom. Money was tight. I felt completely responsible for my young son's future, and I didn't want to rely on someone else's resources for our financial well-being. For the first time in my life, I began to balance my checkbook. Every penny counted.

One day, my sister-in-law told me about a book about money, written by a woman who explained investments in a way everyone could under-stand. Out of sheer necessity, I put aside my fear of numbers and bought the book. And it changed my life.

The book was *Money Dynamics*, by Venita VanCaspel. It may be out of print today, and the tax and investment laws have changed since it was published, but the real message I walked away with from that book is the same message I would like to instill in you: *We do not choose whether or not to play the money game. We all have to. But we do have the choice to learn to play it smart, regardless of our formal training, race, age, or financial status.* Ms. VanCaspel, a woman I've never met, taught me that you don't need to use fancy terms and complex logarithms to set clear goals, establish a financial plan, and evaluate it along the way. Through the use of tables and a handy calculator, I was able to discover the magic of compound interest, and I began to feel in control of my financial life. I would put my four-year-old son to bed at night and sit at the kitchen table to devour the information I knew I could use to ensure a bright future for us.

I was so determined that I decided to start all over and begin again at step one. With my sister-in-law's guidance, I stopped teaching full time and joined the financial planning company for which she worked so that I could learn more about this new world. I started at an entry-level posi-tion, but I worked and studied and took the tests to become a stockbro-ker, and before I knew it, I understood what it took to make money in the stock market.

But how was I going to get clients? A stockbroker without clients is like a party with no guests. So I decided to marry my training with my passion. I was a stockbroker, but in my heart I was still a teacher, so I approached my business from an educational point of view. I held meet-ings in schools and then in local libraries, and with a lesson plan in mind, I made sure that those who attended my seminars walked away with at least one piece of information they didn't have before. I wanted to tempt them to learn more and to hire me as their financial consultant at the same time! I offered to guide them, not making the investment decisions for them, but showing them how to make those decisions for themselves.

Before long, I could not keep up with my workload. It was then that one of the seminar attendees said, "Julie, why don't we start an investment club?" It sounded like fun, although quite honestly I had only a vague idea of what an investment club was. And that's how my business grew beyond my wildest dreams. People of all ages were calling my office because they, too, wanted to be part of an investment club, where with as little as twenty dollars a month, they could learn together how stocks and mutual funds could contribute enormously to their financial lives.

Today, I am happy to say, many new investors have joined the ranks of successful, active traders and mutual fund holders because they have found that the best way to maximize their returns is to learn how to invest in the stock market and in mutual funds.

Just as I have done with those thousands of new investors, now I will share with you how to develop your best investment strategy using all the tools we have at our fingertips today. I'll show you that with mutual funds, your money can work as hard for you as you work for your money.

Mutual funds are like shoes; one size does not fit all. With my special system, you'll learn to choose from among the more than twelve thousand mutual funds out there. You will also discover how to choose those mutual funds that will keep you within your personal range for risk tolerance so you can sleep well at night. I'll show you how to finally understand those statements you receive from your mutual fund companies so you understand where your money is going.

Most importantly, you will learn how to monitor your investments so that you can make sure you're on track with your financial goals. As you approach your financial goals, you may find that you want to adjust your strategy; we'll figure out how to do that together.

I'll show you how to accumulate a nest egg and how to make your nest egg last you for the rest of your life. And you'll be happy to hear that while you are building that nest egg or that account that's going to fund your dreams, you will be able to have a life as well, free from what you may consider the tedious and scary task of keeping up with financial newspapers and daily stock quotes.

Those of you who have a 401(k) at work and, like many, made your investment choices based on the recommendations of the well-meaning person seated next to you in the lunchroom, will find a wealth of information in this book. You'll learn how to maximize the funds in those accounts and make the most profits. I want you to realize how far this basic knowledge can get you, and how your employer and Uncle Sam can both help you achieve your dreams.

In *Fund Your Future* I will teach you how to take control of your financial future so that you don't have to keep fantasizing about hitting the lottery. Instead, you'll be able to enjoy your life while your chauffeur—your mutual fund and your 401(k)—follows the course you have mapped out. You'll get to enjoy the scenery along the way and arrive safely at your desired destination: financial freedom!

It's time to begin our new journey together. Fasten your seat belts; it's going to be a fun ride!

CHAPTER ONE

Before You Can Get Where You're Going, You've Got to Know Where You Are!

I am the worst when it comes to figuring out where I'm going . . . even in my own city! I usually call my husband from the car to ask him how to get to my destination. His first question to me is, "Where are you now?" My answer? "Next to the blue truck and behind the green Honda."

When it comes to money, before we can figure out where we are going, we have to figure out where we are. Do you know where you are in terms of your finances? How much money do you have available to invest? How much money do you really need to reach your goals?

"Whoa! Hold on!" you say. "How can I even consider these questions when I have no money to invest and no way to save any?" If that sounds like you, then we're going to make a little bet. I bet that after you finish the next section, you're going to find that you had more money than you thought. Ready?

Show Me the Money

Our goal here is to identify your most obvious sources of hidden money so that you can begin to apply what's in this book. It's amazing how much faster we can understand this financial stuff when we can see the results step by step, using whatever meager (or not so meager) funds we have to start with. So before we go on to learn how to invest, we need to uncover your hidden assets. And in order to do that, I would like you to get a notebook to use while you read this book, and then answer the following questions. If you'd like to, you may print out this list of Hidden Asset questions from www.JulieStav.com.

1. At the end of each month, after you pay all your bills and right before you get your next check, do you have any money left?

    a. If your answer is yes, what do you do with it? If you save it, are you happy with its rate of return (the interest you are earning on it)? If you are not, circle that amount. This money is a possible investment candidate.

    b. If your answer is no, you are probably forgetting the most important monthly bill you have: *you*! We all tend to live up to—and sometimes even a little beyond—our means. Can you remember the last time you got a raise? It probably either got sucked into the vacuum of bills due, or it seemed to fade into your lifestyle. Usually, the more money we make, the higher our standard of living . . . and the higher our monthly bills.

        If you pay yourself first—*let's say 10 percent of your take-home pay, every single paycheck*—chances are you are still going to cover your monthly expenses as you did before. You may not even miss the 10 percent. Do it. Make it happen. You are your most important financial responsibility, and it's time you take the proper place you deserve: first place! Next paycheck, make out that first check for 10 percent in your name and deposit it into the investment account you are going to start soon. Better yet, do it on payroll deduction directly into your account. We may have already found some money!

2. Are you currently saving or investing money on a regular basis? What is your *rate of return* in this account (how much money is your money generating for you)? Are you happy with its performance? If you're not, circle this amount. If you are happy with its performance, we will still have a use for it later on. Keep it in mind.

3. Do you have a retirement account sitting somewhere? You'd be surprised how many people have taken the first step toward financial freedom by opening an IRA account or participating in their 401(k) at work, only to let their money collect dust at a rate of return of 2 percent or 3 percent because of the uninformed decisions they have made. If this sounds suspiciously like what's happening to you, circle this account.

4. And this one is a doozie: Do you get a tax refund at the end of the year?

    a. If you don't, do you have to pay penalties because you didn't pay enough during the year? If so, keep reading.

    b. If you do get a refund, how much is it? What do you use that money for? (I had a client who overpaid her income taxes by the amount of her car insurance. It was her way of making sure she had the money ready when the bill came in June.) If you are waiting until April each year so you can get some money back from the taxes, you *overpaid*. Do you realize that you are giving Uncle Sam an interest-free loan by using the IRS as a savings account? How much interest did you earn on that refund money while it sat in the government's coffers during the past year? Yep, you got it: zilch, zippo, nada. Circle the amount of your refund.

        I know many of you look forward to getting your tax return. You think of it as freed-up money. ("Yeehaw! $3,000. I can take a vacation!") But, in fact, that $3,000 represents money you loaned to the government—interest-free.

So here is your first tip: If you get more than, say, $300 back as a refund, or if you find yourself paying penalties because you didn't pay enough, call the person who does your taxes. Ask how many withholdings you should be claiming on your paycheck each pay period to enable you to pay your taxes in full by December 31 and perhaps even get a small refund. Once you know how many with-holdings to claim on your paycheck, go to your payroll office and fill out a new W-4 form. This is the official way to tell your payroll office how much money to withdraw from your paycheck and send to the government on your behalf. In your W-4 you will fill out the number of withholdings your tax person advises. This action will reduce the taxes you pay out of your paycheck every pay period and free up more money for you on a monthly basis, ensuring that you do not owe taxes or any penalties at the end of the year. What you have just done is redirect some money to *you* rather than have Uncle Sam keep it until April when you do your taxes.

The ideal situation is to have you come out just even. (By the way, if you set up an automatic savings transfer from your payroll directly to your investment account with the extra money you were sending to the government, come next April, you will have your refund amount *plus* the profit from interest on that refund available to you!)

5. Now, what about your little "secret stash"? Yes, don't look at me with that innocent face. Most of us have a little money socked away for a rainy day, money that nobody knows about. Draw a secret circle around that one, too! If you're going to hide some bucks, you might as well make them grow!

6. Do you have change in your purse or pants pockets or scattered around your car or office? Get a coffee can. Every night, right before you get to bed, empty your coins into the can. You'd be surprised how much money you can accumulate at the end of each month.

7. Are you holding on to old life insurance policies, stocks that were passed on to you by well-intentioned relatives, your children's savings bonds? Can you vaguely remember where you keep them? Get them out and dust them off. You may have found the beginning of your investment nest egg.

8. Tidbits here and there: Is there any other possible source of money I have not asked you about? Look in your file cabinets, shuffle through your desk drawers, and rifle through old tax returns. Have you forgotten anything?

9. Now comes the killer question: Is there anything you can do to save more money than you are currently saving?

If this sounds like I am forcing you to put yourself on a budget, let me tell you a story that may help you look at things a little differently.

Most people think that they have to start from ground zero to begin saving money. Wrong! Sometimes it's simply about looking at the money you already have in a different way.

Twenty years ago, I was at my lowest point financially. I had a mortgage, a four-year-old child to support, a low-paying job, and no savings. I imagined that I had no money to spend on anything. So, poor me, I used to spend lots of time every weekend going to swap meets "just to look" at all the delectably tempting junk. Who knew when I might uncover a truly worthy piece of furniture or china? Then I realized that I was spending quite a bit of money on my seemingly innocent weekend pastime—about $1,000 a year, to be exact! That's nearly $100 per month! When I saw that I could move that $1,000 from the cashier's box at the swap meets into a mutual fund account instead, and in a while, afford to buy that furniture or china new, I was willing to budget just a bit.

"But I hate to budget!" you cry. I agree with you! Completely! Budgeting is the practice of tallying each bloody cent of your income and every little expense every single month and then adjusting your spending in proportion to your income. For many people, this process really works. These people probably also have the willpower to pass on that succulent chocolate soufflé at the end of a heavy meal. This book is for those of us who can't.

Yet there is something about budgeting that does put you on the road to success and that is this: Budgeting helps you to get your financial priorities in order. (What would you rather have: twelve pieces of used swap-meet furniture or a rapidly growing investment account that can pay for your dream retirement?) And you don't need to count every darn penny and compare it to every dang cent you make every month, either. But you do need to look at your overall spending patterns and see if you can come up with your own swap-meet examples. Because there is one thing that I found out about myself that seems to apply to most people: We all continue to spend aimlessly until we are presented with a better alternative.

That said, I am certainly not going to force you to budget. I am not going to force you to do anything. Go on, keep spending! As long as spending is more enjoyable than investing or even thinking about money, you are going to shop or travel or do whatever it is that brings you pleasure, even if it is sinking you into a sea of debt, persistent depression, and financial disarray. As anyone who has ever struggled to overcome an addiction or an unpleasant personality quirk knows: No one can make you do anything until you are ready. And no one likes a bully, so I am not going there, either.

The good news is that I have discovered a better way than forcing you to budget. And I have my children to thank for it.

How do you get a four-year-old to stop watching his favorite television show? You know, the one with the gory scenes of monsters and dragons that you are sure you'll have to deal with when he shows up at your bedside at 3:00 A.M. because he had a nightmare? Well, you could block that channel (pretty drastic, Big Brother!). You could forbid the activity (and have to deal with a screaming, crying demon-child!). You could try to explain the merits of watching educational television instead. (Yeah right, what planet do *you* live on?) Or you could offer an alternative that is more appealing to him than the one he is engaging in. How about baking cookies with Mom? Going to the park with the dog? Watching a new video? You can get very creative and, with a little luck, your preschooler may take the lead and engage in the new activity while not feeling deprived or punished for having given up the old one.

Just as we craftily got the young person to delight in the rewards of mastering something new, I want to tempt you with the rewards of getting your investment house in order. So answer that last question fearlessly: Is there anything else you can do to put aside a bit more while putting yourself on the road to success?

At this point, I probably win the bet: You have learned where you have money you didn't know you had. Good! You've already completed the first step in my system. Now you know where you are. Later on in this book, I am going to show you how these hidden assets will make a *big* difference in bringing you closer to your investment goals.

But first you need to figure out where you want to go with what you've got. That's our next stop on your moneymaking journey.

CHAPTER TWO

Taking the First Steps

Remember when you were five years old, how easy it was to answer the question, "What do you want to be when you grow up?" Out of your mouth came answers such as: "I'm going to be a pilot and a fireman and a teacher and a construction worker and a doctor and a . . ." My son Tony wanted to be a garbage collector. When I asked him why he had chosen that profession, he quickly answered, "Because they only have to work one day a week!" Now there's a kid who knew what he wanted!

When we were children, fantasizing about the future was an exciting pastime, but goal-setting as grown-ups can seem like a daunting task. However, with a little practice and a simple checklist, you will rediscover the enchantment of looking into the future with a sense of anticipation and a can-do feeling. You will learn what it takes to make your grown-up dreams come true.

The Pot at the End of the Rainbow

Financial goals are specific milestones we set for ourselves. We all have our dreams and wishes, but without specific and attainable objectives, we are doomed to wander aimlessly without a definite course.

Financial goals come in many shapes and sizes. A financial goal may be to accumulate a single lump sum of money you wish to have for a specific purpose sometime in the future. It may be to amass money toward a down payment on a home or to build a retirement nest egg from which you will draw your future income.

No matter what your goal is, the process is the same. In goal setting, there are five steps.

Step 1. State Your Goal in Specific, Positive Language

If your first financial goal is to get out of debt, rather than saying, "I want to be debt free," you may want to rephrase that statement with something like, "I want to pay off my two highest-rate credit cards by the end of next year." This latter statement gives you a clearer picture of where you are going because you are stating a specific, measurable purpose.

You may wish to have enough money for a two-week Caribbean cruise, a down payment for a home, a college education fund for your children, or just some cold, hard cash to buy a luxury car. Whatever your specific financial desires may be, jot them down in your notebook. That's the first step on your road to financial achievement!

Step 2. How Much Money Will You Need?

Once you have determined your specific goal, write down how much money you will need to achieve it. You need to know specifically how much money will be required.

You should be able to measure your goal and monitor your progress, so state your goal in dollars and cents. If your goal is to fund a vacation account or some other one-time purchase, do your homework and write down how much money you will need to have for that purpose. You can always adjust the amount. What's important now is that you set a measurable challenge.

But wait a minute! What if your goal is to pay off a loan or credit card debt? You might owe $1,000 today, but every month they're adding interest. How do you figure out the specific amount you need if this amount keeps changing? Don't sweat it. If this is your situation, just go to the end of this chapter, where I explain it all.

Or what if your goal is to amass a nest egg—a retirement fund—from which you'll draw a monthly income? That introduces a whole other set of issues. But do not worry, it's nothing we can't figure out together. I'll walk you through that process in the next chapter.

Step 3. When Do You Want to Accomplish Your Goal?

Set a specific date by which you want to achieve your goal. To help you do this, you may find it helpful to organize your goals into three categories:

1. Short-term goals, of which there are two types: Those that you wish to reach in two years or less, and those you have two to five years to achieve. The first type does not count as investment money because you do not have time to make a substantial profit. The second type does provide enough time. We will cover both in this book.

2. Goals that you are planning to achieve in a period of five to ten years. These are our medium-term goals.

3. Long-term goals are those that you wish to accomplish in ten or more years.

You don't need to have goals in each of these categories. Perhaps you have a clear picture in your mind of what you wish to accomplish in the short term. Maybe you have set your mind on achieving a long-term dream. Or you may have different goals that fall into one or more of these categories. *You can use the system you learn in this book to help you achieve* all *of your different financial goals.* And my wish for you is that as time goes by and you begin to increase the return on your investments and your knowledge of investing principles, you begin to achieve your goals sooner than you expected. Wouldn't that be marvelous!

Step 4. How Much Money Do You Have Already Set Aside Toward Your Goal?

Now that you have established what you want to achieve financially and when you wish to reach your goal, take a look at your savings and existing investments (if any), and see how much of that money you can allocate to the attainment of that goal. Remember your hidden assets and the money you found there? This is where you begin to make it work for you. The more you have already put aside toward your objective, the easier it will be to achieve it.

Step 5. How Much Money Do You Need to Invest on a Monthly Basis to Make Sure You Accomplish Your Goal?

The last step in goal-setting is determining how much money you need to set aside each month to reach your goal. If the amount you have already managed to save is enough to get you to where you want to go, you do not need to add any additional money on a monthly basis toward that goal. Good for you! You can instead invest on a monthly basis toward a different goal. If you don't know how to figure out this step, keep reading; we're going to have a practice run at figuring it all out.

Let's Try It on for Size

Now that you have the steps that you need to set your financial goals, let's go through an example together. In this scenario, we'll be using a short-term goal, i.e., working toward a lump sum of money to be used all at once within two years or less.

Our first step is to state the goal in specific and positive terms. Let's pretend that you want to go on a two-week vacation to Tahiti. Take your notebook and write steps 1 through 5 in a column, and write "two-week vacation to Tahiti" next to step 1. You may also print out this Five-Step Financial Goal Checklist from www.JulieStav.com.

> **STEP 1: Stated goal** 2-week vacation to Tahiti
>
> **STEP 2: Cost of goal**
>
> **STEP 3: Years till goal**
>
> **STEP 4: $ available now**
>
> **STEP 5: Monthly amount needed**

Our next step is to determine how much money you will need for this purpose. Let's say that after excitedly perusing travel brochures about Tahiti, you decided to splurge on your vacation and your two-week get-away will cost you about $4,700. To be safe, plan on having $5,000. Write $5,000 next to step 2.

> **STEP 1: Stated goal** 2-week vacation to Tahiti
>
> **STEP 2: Cost of goal** $5,000
>
> **STEP 3: Years till goal**
>
> **STEP 4: $ available now**
>
> **STEP 5: Monthly amount needed**

In step 3, you set a time limit of when you wish to achieve your financial goal. You want to be able to afford to go to Tahiti two years from today. Write down two years next to step 3.

> **STEP 1: Stated goal** 2-week vacation to Tahiti
>
> **STEP 2: Cost of goal** $5,000
>
> **STEP 3: Years till goal** 2 years

STEP 4: $ available now

STEP 5: Monthly amount needed

Let's assume that you have $500 already set aside for your trip to Tahiti. This money has been sitting in a savings account for some time now, and you are going to use it in two years for your trip. Write $500 next to step 4.

STEP 1: Stated goal 2-week vacation to Tahiti

STEP 2: Cost of goal $5,000

STEP 3: Years till goal 2 years

STEP 4: $ available now $500

STEP 5: Monthly amount needed

Before you go on to the final step, you will want to know how that $500 will grow in two years. That amount will go toward your vacation goal of $5,000.

If that money is hidden in your underwear drawer, at the end of two years, you'll just have that $500. But let's assume you put that money in the bank and are currently earning 5 percent interest in your savings account. (If you are earning 5 percent or less in your short-term savings account or CD, don't worry; in later chapters you will learn how to increase the return on your money for short-term investments of two to five years. Once you know how to choose the best investments, you will demand a better interest rate on all your money.)

For the math lovers: you could take a calculator, multiply $500 by .05 (this will give you the interest earned on your $500 after one year). Take this amount, add it to your original $500 to figure out how much you will have in total after one year. Then multiply that amount by .05 to figure out how much interest you will earn after two years. Add this to your first-year total. It looks like this:

$500 \times .05 = \$25$

$\$25 + \$500 = \$525$ (end of year 1)

$\$525 \times .05 = \$26.25$

$\$26.25 + \$525 = \$551.25$ (end of year 2)

Or, for those of you who hate math, you can toss your calculator, save your energy, and just use the following table to determine the future value of that $500 at 5 percent interest.

FUTURE VALUE OF A $1 INVESTMENT AT VARYING RATES OF RETURN

Years to Goal	Average Annual Interest Earned								
	5%	6%	7%	8%	9%	10%	11%	12%	15%
35	$5.52	$7.69	$10.68	$14.79	$20.41	$28.10	$38.58	$52.80	$133.18
30	$4.32	$5.74	$7.61	$10.06	$13.27	$17.45	$22.89	$29.96	$66.21
25	$3.39	$4.29	$5.43	$6.85	$8.62	$10.84	$13.59	$17.00	$32.92
20	$2.65	$3.21	$3.87	$4.66	$5.60	$6.73	$8.06	$9.65	$16.37
15	$2.08	$2.40	$2.76	$3.17	$3.64	$4.18	$4.79	$5.47	$8.14
10	$1.63	$1.79	$1.97	$2.16	$2.37	$2.59	$2.84	$3.11	$4.05
5	$1.28	$1.34	$1.40	$1.47	$1.54	$1.61	$1.69	$1.76	$2.01
4	$1.22	$1.26	$1.31	$1.36	$1.41	$1.46	$1.52	$1.57	$1.75
3	$1.16	$1.19	$1.23	$1.26	$1.30	$1.33	$1.37	$1.40	$1.52
2	$1.10	$1.12	$1.15	$1.17	$1.19	$1.21	$1.23	$1.25	$1.32

Find the column that shows how many years you have to reach your goal, in this case, two years. Now run your finger to the right until you reach the column under 5 percent. The number there is $1.10. Notice, though, that this table shows the balance of your account if you had a $1 starting amount. Since you had $500, you need to multiply $1.10 by 500. The result is $550. In two years, at 5 percent interest, your account will have grown to $550. (This chart is not as accurate as doing the math yourself, but the difference is only $1, and for the amount of work this chart saves, that's close enough.) Save this number for now; you'll need it in calculating step 5.

The final step is to determine how much money you are going to need to save on a monthly basis to reach your $5,000.

In step 4, you found that your current savings account of $500 will be worth $550 in two years. Subtract that amount from the $5,000 needed to pay for your vacation.

$$\$5,000-\$550 = \$4,450$$

So we need to figure out how much money you need to set aside on a monthly basis to reach $4,450.

Take a look at the following table. It gives us the monthly investment needed to reach a $1,000 goal.

MONTHLY INVESTMENT NEEDED TO REACH A $1,000 GOAL

Years to Goal	Average Annual Interest Earned								
	5%	6%	7%	8%	9%	10%	11%	12%	15%
35	$.88	$.70	$.56	$.44	$.34	$.26	$.20	$.16	$.07
30	$1.20	$1.00	$.82	$.67	$.55	$.44	$.36	$.29	$.14
25	$1.68	$1.44	$1.23	$1.05	$.89	$.75	$.63	$.53	$.31
20	$2.43	$2.16	$1.92	$1.70	$1.50	$1.32	$1.16	$1.01	$.67
15	$3.74	$3.44	$3.15	$2.89	$2.64	$2.41	$2.20	$2.00	$1.50
10	$6.44	$6.10	$5.78	$5.47	$5.17	$4.88	$4.61	$4.35	$3.63
5	$14.70	$14.33	$13.97	$13.61	$13.26	$12.91	$12.58	$12.24	$11.29
4	$18.78	$18.39	$18.00	$17.63	$17.26	$16.89	$16.53	$16.17	$15.14
3	$25.70	$25.30	$24.90	$24.51	$24.12	$23.74	$23.36	$22.98	$21.89
2	$39.70	$40.00	$39.32	$38.94	$38.56	$38.18	$37.81	$37.44	$36.34

Since you wish to reach your goal in two years, find that number under the Years to Goal column. Assuming that you earn 5 percent on your monthly savings, find the figure under the column for 5 percent. That number is $39.70. That is the amount of money you would need to save on a monthly basis to reach $1,000 in two years at 5 percent interest.

"But that's not enough!" you say. "I need $4,450, not just $1,000." You're right! Your goal is about four and a half times $1,000. So in order to use the handy table on page 23, which uses thousands, we first need to divide your lump sum amount (which is $4,450) by 1,000.

$$\$4,450 \div 1,000 = 4.45$$

Now multiply this number times $39.70 to get to your monthly investment.

$$\$39.70 \times 4.45 = \$176.67$$

You need to set aside $176.67 every month for two years to achieve your vacation goal. Tahiti, here you come!

STEP 1: Stated goal 2-week vacation to Tahiti

STEP 2: Cost of goal $5,000

STEP 3: Years till goal 2 years

STEP 4: $ available now $500 ($511 in 2 years at 5% interest)

STEP 5: Monthly amount needed $176.67

Let's Go for Another Lap Around the Track

Here's another example that's only slightly more complicated. Let's run through the five steps again, only this time, the goal is to save for four years of college for your child. With college funds, you add up the total amount of money you will need for the four years, and you aim to reach that goal at the *beginning of the first year* that your child is due to attend college.

Take out your notebook again, and write down the five steps. The first step is to write down what your specific goal is. You are saving toward four years of college tuition. Write it down next to step 1. Your list should look like this:

STEP 1: Stated goal   4 years of college tuition

STEP 2: Cost of goal

STEP 3: Years till goal

STEP 4: $ available now

STEP 5: Monthly amount needed

The next step is to write down your goal amount. Let's assume that tuition is expected to be $10,000 a year by the time your son or daughter attends school. Since you are saving for a four-year college, you will need $40,000 to cover the expenses of all four years, so write down $40,000 next to step 2.

STEP 1: Stated goal   4 years of college tuition

STEP 2: Cost of goal $40,000

STEP 3: Years till goal

STEP 4: $ available now

STEP 5: Monthly amount needed

The next step is to write down how many years you have to accomplish your goal. If your child is two years old, you will have approximately fifteen years to add to the college fund. Write down that number next to step 3.

STEP 1: Stated goal   4 years of college tuition

STEP 2: Cost of goal $40,000

STEP 3: Years till goal   15

STEP 4: $ available now

STEP 5: Monthly amount needed

Now that you have established your goal in specific terms and the number of years you have to accomplish it, do you have any existing accounts that could be used for this purpose? If you do, write down the amount you have available in step 4. We will assume that you already have $1,000 in a college fund.

STEP 1: Stated goal   4 years of college tuition

STEP 2: Cost of goal $40,000

STEP 3: Years till goal   15

STEP 4: $ available now $1,000

STEP 5: Monthly amount needed

Now we need to see how that $1,000 will grow over the next fifteen years. Once we find out how much that account will be worth in fifteen years, we can subtract that number from our goal of $40,000. *The difference will be the amount we need to achieve, with our monthly investments, between now and our future goal date.* Remember which table to use? If you said that we needed to use the Future Value of a $1 table on page 22 in this chapter, you are absolutely right. That is the table that will help you project the future value of an existing account.

But this time, let's assume an 8 percent rate of return on our money, just as a hypothetical example. Find the number fifteen under the Years to Goal column. Now run your finger to the right until you reach the column under 8 percent. That number is $3.17. One dollar earning

8 percent will grow to $3.17 in fifteen years. One thousand dollars will grow to $3,170 over the next fifteen years at 8 percent.

$$\$3.17 \times 1,000 = \$3,170$$

This account will give you a nice head start toward your $40,000 goal, so go ahead and subtract it from your end total.

$$\$40,000 - \$3,170 = \$36,830$$

Your next and final step is to find out how much money you need to set aside to reach $36,830 in fifteen years. We will assume the same 8 percent rate of return.

The Monthly Investment table on page 23 is the tool that will help us arrive at the monthly investment needed to reach our goal in the future.

Find fifteen under Years to Goal, and move your finger to the right under 8 percent. The number there is 2.89. That means that, in order to have $1,000 in your account fifteen years from now, you need to save $2.89 per month. Huh? What is wrong with that picture? $1,000 would probably only buy your college-bound youngster a one-semester parking permit. We need $36,830, not $1,000! So to get that big number, divide 36,830 by 1,000.

$$\$36,830 \div 1,000 = 36.830$$

Now multiply that number times 2.89.

$$\$36.830 \times 2.89 = \$106.44$$

You will need to set aside $106.44 each month at 8 percent over the next fifteen years to have your $40,000 available for college tuition. Your finished chart should look like this:

STEP 1: Stated goal   4 years of college tuition

STEP 2: Cost of goal $40,000

STEP 3: Years till goal   15

STEP 4: $ available now $1,000 ($3,170 in 15 yrs at 8%)

STEP 5: Monthly amount needed $106.44

Digging Yourself Out of a Credit Card Debt Hole

"This all sounds great," you say. But under your breath you whisper that you would just be happy to get out of debt. Well, there's help for that, too.

Credit card companies make their money by charging you interest on the amount you owe. They make it very easy for you to carry a balance from month to month, rather than pay your loan off in full when the bill arrives. The longer you keep that tab open, the more money they make off you.

For example, if you owed $1,000 total on a credit card, and you only paid the minimum payment of 2 percent or $20 per month, do you know how much you would end up paying that credit card company in the end? Hold on to your hats; this gets really ugly.

If your yearly interest is 13 percent, your total payments would add up to $1,420, and it would take you seventy-one months (that's almost six years!) to pay it off. A huge rip-off, right?

Wait, it gets even uglier.

What if your yearly interest is 21 percent, which many credit card companies typically charge? Your total payments would be $2,260 (that's more than twice the original amount you borrowed) and it would take you 113 months to liquidate your debt (that's over nine years!). Big, fat, gross rip-off!

So if your goal is to pay off your credit card debt, this is what you need to do:

1. Cut up all of your credit cards except for the one with the lowest interest rate charge, which you will keep for emergencies only. Start

telling yourself that you will not spend what you cannot see in your checking account or in green in your wallet.[1]

2. Find out your card's yearly interest rate on the left-hand side of the following table, and move across the top to the time you would like to pay it off in—the sooner the better, you have better things to spend your money on! The box that coincides with these two numbers is the amount you need to pay monthly in order to pay off $1,000 debt.

MONTHLY AMOUNT NEEDED TO PAY OFF $1,000 IN CREDIT CARD DEBT

Annual Interest rate being charged	Years to pay off your debt				
	1	2	3	4	5
9%	$86.80	$45.34	$31.56	$24.70	$20.60
10%	$87.19	$45.76	$32.00	$25.15	$21.07
11%	$87.58	$46.18	$32.44	$25.61	$21.54
12%	$87.97	$46.61	$32.89	$26.07	$22.02
13%	$88.36	$47.03	$33.33	$26.54	$22.51
14%	$88.75	$47.46	$33.78	$27.01	$23.00
15%	$89.14	$47.89	$34.24	$27.49	$23.50
16%	$89.54	$48.32	$34.69	$27.97	$24.00
17%	$89.93	$48.75	$35.15	$28.45	$24.51
18%	$90.33	$49.19	$35.62	$28.94	$25.02
19%	$90.72	$49.62	$36.08	$29.43	$25.54
20%	$91.12	$50.06	$36.55	$29.93	$26.06
21%	$91.51	$50.50	$37.03	$30.43	$26.59

[1]If the one credit card you save for emergencies still has a high interest rate I suggest you do some research on how to get one with a lower rate. You can start by calling your credit card companies and threatening to cut up the card if they can't significantly improve the rate. You can also save all those notices you receive in the mail—don't forget to read the small print, especially the information about when that "introductory low rate" may expire. Another option is to check online. Go to lowcards.com or type in *cheap credit cards* in your search engine.

Let's say your credit card company charges 21 percent interest, and you want to pay off your debt in three years. You find 21 percent in the left-hand column, and run your finger across until you are under the column for three years. The number there is $37. You need to pay $37 a month to pay off your $1,000 debt in three years.

Now, if you owe more than $1,000, divide what you owe by 1,000. Let's say you owe $5,000:

$$\$5,000 \div 1,000 = 5$$

Now multiply your monthly payment by five.

$$\$37 \times 5 = \$185$$

You will need to pay $185 each month for three years in order to pay off your $5,000 credit card debt.

This is what your five-step chart would end up looking like if you go through this process the way we have outlined it:

STEP 1: Stated goal Pay off credit card debt

STEP 2: Cost of goal $5,000 at 21%

STEP 3: Years till goal 3

STEP 4: $ available now 0

STEP 5: Monthly amount needed $185 ($37 × 5)

Take charge of your future by not working for the credit card company. Make a commitment to a monthly amount, and next time they ask you, "Cash or credit?" leave the plastic in your wallet.

Let's Recap

Want to pinpoint your financial dreams? Follow the five-step system:

STEP 1. Write down what you want and state it in a positive, concise manner.

STEP 2. Give your goal a dollar amount. This step will help you see your dream more clearly.

STEP 3. Determine how long you are willing to wait until you reach your goal.

STEP 4. Find any possible resources you may already have that could be put to use toward your purpose.

STEP 5. Establish how much money you need to set aside per month to achieve your dream.

You can follow the steps in this chapter to help you accomplish any lump-sum financial goal you may have.

Your purpose may be short-term, such as paying off credit card debt; medium-term, such as investing toward a down payment for a home; or long-term, such as funding your retirement. You now have the tools you need to project the growth of an existing account and to establish a monthly investment program to reach a desired future amount. By following the five steps you have learned in this chapter, you have drawn your personal road map to success. You will feel more in control of your financial destiny. And you will sleep better at night knowing that your money is going where you want it to go.

Once you have done all this planning, work with a vengeance toward your goal. Commit to putting aside the money you need to reach your target, and do not allow yourself to veer off track. Your diligence will be compensated with the sweet reward of reaching your desired financial destination.

The examples we just went through were scenarios in which your investments were to be cashed out in one lump sum or in which you had to pay monthly money to reach your goals. We also assumed rates of return of 5 percent or more. You may currently have accounts with smaller interest rates, but when you are done with this book, you will have kissed your tiny interest rates good-bye, especially when it comes to your medium- and long-term goals. You will be able to achieve interest rates on your money that will bring you much better results on your investments much faster.

In the next chapter, I will show you how to set realistic retirement goals to build a long-term nest egg that will provide you with enough monthly income so you can stop working for a living. Golf, anyone?

CHAPTER THREE

Funding Your Dreams

In the fable of the ants and the grasshopper, we first meet the ants when the autumn air is beginning to turn chilly, and the leaves are starting to fall off the trees. The little ants have been working diligently since spring and all through the summer, gathering grain for the coming winter. They work day and night, taking breaks only in shifts. They urge their friend, the grasshopper, to do the same while he still has time, but he can't be bothered. It is more tempting to sleep late, bask in the waning sun, and glory in the new moon. Then winter hits. The ants have it made; they get to enjoy indoor dining during the snowy winter storms. But the grasshopper, who had idled away his days, never thinking about the future, must stay out in the cold, begging for measly leftovers to survive.

In my twenty years of experience in the field of financial planning, I have come across many ants and many grasshoppers. Some of my clients worked day and night preparing for the time when they either could not continue or would not want to continue working. Others seemed to think that it would all work out somehow; after all, they were contributing to their 401(k) at work.

You don't need to work as hard as those industrious ants, but you do need to prepare for the future so that you don't wind up freezing your you-know-what off when the future suddenly becomes the present.

In chapter 2, we followed five specific steps that guided us through the process of achieving a specific financial goal on a specific deadline. The five steps you learned are useful for establishing short-, medium-, and long-term goals that require having access to a lump sum of money or paying off a lump-sum debt.

In this chapter, we are going to add a new twist to the process. This time, we are not just saving for a lump sum that we will use all at once. Our goal here is to build a nest egg that will provide us with the income we wish to receive on a *monthly basis* for all of our retirement years.

Retiring comfortably means simply being able to stop working for a living and yet continue to receive a monthly income that will allow us to satisfy our ongoing needs and newfound lifestyle.

Long gone are the images of a sedate, mature person who is winding down at the end of a life's journey and who no longer has the ability to work. We are living longer and more productive lives. Retirement doesn't mean sitting at home waiting to die. It could mean traveling cross-country in an RV; taking up golf and playing the best and most challenging courses in the world; or maybe it's going back to school to pursue the course of study you've always dreamed about.

Whatever you decide to spend your time doing, there is also no set age for retirement. Ideally, the sooner you are able to stop working and still generate your desired monthly income, the better. If you wish to continue working after that point or perhaps even start a new business or change careers, more power to you, but it will be a conscious decision based on your personal desires rather than on financial necessity.

Many of my associates in the field of financial planning may profess that you will need between 70 and 80 percent of your current income after retirement. I don't agree. Why should we work so hard throughout our lives looking forward to the day when we get to *decrease* our standard of living? When we think of retirement, we should envision a *better* life than we have today, and that may mean more income than we have today. With the right planning, we can fulfill our dreams of the future, whatever they are.

Retirement financial planning is the process of projecting ahead what our needs, wants, and desires may be and establishing a plan that will allow us to accumulate enough money to create a nest egg. That nest egg should be large enough to provide the monthly income you will need just from the interest it makes.

"Retirement planning sounds good," you say, "but where do I begin? It's hard enough to plan my next summer vacation. How am I supposed to know what I'll need at retirement?" You're right. Retirement planning *can* be overwhelming. But it doesn't *have* to be. I'll help you get started, and I'll walk you through the steps.

Working Hard Is Not Enough, You've Got to Work Smart

Every dollar you set aside for your future can act as a self-generating money machine that continues to increase your money without any laborious effort on your part. You will need to prepare only once, set the wheels in motion, and then enjoy your well-deserved rest, all thanks to one of the most important concepts of investing: *compound interest*. Let me explain.

If you deposited $1,000 in a savings account and you earned 5 percent on it, at the end of the first year, you would have $1,050. That $50 represents the *profit* or interest you have earned on your money during the first year. If you resisted the temptation to withdraw any money from your account and left it alone for another year at the same interest rate, you would earn 5 percent interest not on your original deposit of $1,000 but instead on the $1,050 you had at the beginning of the second year. You are earning interest on interest, as well as on your *principal* (your original deposit). Your account balance at the end of the second year would be $1,050 plus 5 percent on that amount, or $1,102.50.

This Compound Interest table shows you how that $1,000 would grow over time at 5 percent without your having to add any additional deposits. Your initial deposit is just accruing interest on top of interest, year after year. This is the real power of investing: to generate enough profit on your money so your money begins to work as hard for you as you worked for the original amount you invested.

ORIGINAL DEPOSIT OF $1,000 EARNING 5% INTEREST

Years	End of Year Balance	Gain for That Year
1	$1,050	$50.00
2	$1,102.50	$52.50
3	$1,157.63	$55.13
4	$1,215.51	$57.88
5	$1,276.28	$60.77
10	$1,628.89	$77.56
15	$2,078.93	$99.00
20	$2,653.30	$126.35
25	$3,386.35	$161.25

As you can see from this table, you are getting a "raise" every year in the amount you are earning on your savings, all with no effort on your part, aside from leaving the money in the account. This is how money is made in investments, by earning interest on interest.

Compound interest has no minimum requirement in order to work. Your investment, large or small, can pick up tremendous speed with the effects of this mathematical wonder. Compound interest is the magic that takes no coffee breaks, no vacation, and no sick days. It is the most powerful tool for making your money multiply, and all it takes is an initial amount of money, a decent *rate of return* (the money your money makes if it's left alone to grow), and a little time.

Remember, successful investing is not so much a question of "timing" but a question of "time *in*," meaning the amount of time the money and its profits are left, *untouched*, in the account.

So when it comes to investing toward a cushy retirement, you are not working alone. You can use the power of compound interest so that, instead of preparing for retirement as if it were a cold winter ahead, you can be ready for a joyful and carefree period of your life with tons of free time to devote to your hobbies, your family, your faith—whatever your heart desires.

How Much Money Will You Need?

I want you to picture yourself during your retirement years being able to spend your time any way you want. Think of where you would want to live and the kinds of activities you would like to enjoy. Now I want you to answer the following question: How much money would you need on a monthly basis to be able to feel comfortable and secure in that dream environment if you were able to retire today? The answer to that question is the first step on your way to preparing for a secure and joyful retirement. Take out your notebook and pencil, and write the steps from 1 to 7 (you can print out the Seven Steps to Retirement Checklist at www.JulieStav.com).

Begin your list by writing the amount of money you would like to bring home every month to feel financially comfortable and secure. Be nice to yourself. Don't skimp here. Let's assume that you would need to bring home $3,000 a month if you were to retire today. Your list so far would look like this:

Step 1: Desired monthly income $3,000

Step 2:

Step 3:

Step 4:

Step 5:

Step 6:

Step 7:

How Many Years Until Retirement?

Once you have arrived at your desired monthly income, the next step is to set a specific date by which you wish to reach your goal. If you are thirty-five years old and you wish to explore retiring at sixty-five, you will have another thirty years to work toward your goal and accumulate enough money to retire in style. Add step 2 to your list like this:

Step 1: Desired monthly income $3,000

Step 2: Years to goal 30

Step 3:

Step 4:

Step 5:

Step 6:

Step 7:

Take Inflation into Account

Your $3,000 a month thirty years from now will not buy you the same goods and services it buys you today.

Every year, the prices of food, clothing, shelter, and transportation go up. In 1940, for example, you could buy ten loaves of bread for a dollar. By 1950, you could buy only six loaves. How many loaves of bread can you buy today with a dollar? I don't know where you shop, but at my local bakery, a dollar wouldn't even get me half a loaf of day-old bread.

The name for that creeping up of prices over time is *inflation*. It is a fact of life.

Let's assume that inflation increases at an average rate of 3 percent over the next thirty years. The average inflation in the past has been approximately 3 percent a year, and this is also the figure that experts are projecting into the future. So we will use 3 percent for our example. Every year that goes by you would need to have 3 percent more money to buy the same goods and services you bought the year before. That may not seem like much, but just to give you an example of how inflation affects the buying power of our money, listen to this: If you had $100 to spend today, and we averaged 3 percent inflation a year for the next thirty years, thirty years from today, you would need to have $242.70 to buy what $100 would buy you now.

If you don't adjust your desired monthly amount by the inflation factor, you are going to come up very short. So we need to project the *equivalent* of our desired monthly income of $3,000 thirty years into the future. How do we do that?

Use the following Inflation Table to find out how much your desired monthly income will need to be in the future after accounting for inflation. Since the exact rate of future inflation is unpredictable, I provide you with the range of inflation between 2 percent and 5 percent.

INFLATION TABLE

Number of Years	Average Inflation Rate Per Year			
	2	3	4	5
5	1.104	1.159	1.217	1.276
10	1.219	1.344	1.480	1.629
15	1.346	1.558	1.801	2.079
20	1.486	1.806	2.191	2.653
25	1.641	2.094	2.666	3.386
30	1.811	2.427	3.243	4.322

Since we are assuming a retirement date thirty years from today, and a 3 percent inflation rate per year between now and then, place your finger at thirty years and move it to the right until you reach the column under 3 percent. You will see the number 2.427. This means that in thirty years, you will need 2.427 times the amount you require today. So take your desired monthly amount and multiply it times 2.427. The result will be your equivalent monthly income in the future.

$$\$3,000 \times 2.427 = \$7,281$$

Add this line to our list, which should now look like this:

Step 1: Desired monthly income $3,000

Step 2: Years to goal   30

Step 3: Monthly income needed after inflation $7,281

Step 4:

Step 5:

Step 6:

Step 7:

"Oh my! $7,281!" you cry. "How on earth am I going to get ahead, if inflation keeps eating away at my nest egg year after year?"

By choosing investments whose returns exceed the rate of inflation. From 1926 to 1999, inflation rose at an average of 3 percent. During the same period, stocks in the United States had an average annual return of 11 percent. We can't say the same for savings accounts or bonds. They barely stayed up with the rate of inflation. Studies show that in the future, stocks are expected to average an annual return of 11.6 percent, while savings accounts projections show an average of 4.5 percent. Inflation is expected to remain at approximately 3 percent. You tell me which is the better choice.

Not yet convinced? Let's go to the next step.

Other Sources of Income

Once you have projected your future equivalent monthly income, your next step is to look for any other source of income that you are expecting to receive during retirement. You may have a pension from work, income from rental property, or a trust in your name. Perhaps you are planning to continue to work part time. Subtract any source of *monthly* income—income that you can reasonably expect to continue to receive monthly—from your desired monthly amount. The end result will be the income you will need to generate each month from your investment accounts. Put this adjusted amount in the list for step 4. In our example, we will assume that you are not expecting any other monthly income at retirement. Your list now looks like this:

Step 1: Desired monthly income $3,000

Step 2: Years to goal 30

Step 3: Monthly income needed after inflation $7,281

Step 4: Adjusted monthly income needed (step 3 minus other monthly income) $7,281

Step 5:

Step 6:

Step 7:

Note: If you know the monthly amount of Social Security income you will be receiving, subtract it from the total you will require in step 4. The result will be the amount you will use for the rest of the process. You may request a statement from Social Security showing your estimated benefits at retirement. It is called a Request for Earnings and Benefit Estimate Statement (Form SSA-7004-SM), and it's available online at www.ssa.gov. You may also call the Social Security Administration at (800) 772-1213 and ask that a form be sent to you.

How Big of a Nest Egg Will You Need?

Once you have subtracted any other sources of monthly retirement income from your projected amount, you will need to find out how much money in dollars and cents you must have so you can receive your monthly "retirement paycheck" from this account, *indefinitely, for as long as you live.*

The following Nest Egg calculator table will help you project the lump-sum amount you will need at retirement time to provide you with

NEST EGG NEEDED TO PROVIDE DESIRED MONTHLY INCOME DURING RETIREMENT

If You Are Receiving This Rate of Return	Multiply Your Desired Monthly Amount Times This Number
3%	400
4%	300
5%	240
6%	200
7%	171.43
8%	150
9%	133.33
10%	120
11%	109.09
12%	100
13%	92.31
14%	85.71
15%	80
20%	60
25%	48
30%	40

your desired income. We will assume that at retirement you will be able to receive an 8 percent annual rate of return. This number may seem high to you now, but after reading this book, I am sure that you will demand that your money work harder for you than it has in the past.

Find 8 percent on the left column, and multiply your desired monthly amount times the number next to 8 percent (150). In our example, we are multiplying $7,281 × 150 = $1,092,150. Let's add this figure to our list like this:

Step 1: Desired monthly income $3,000

Step 2: Years to goal   30

Step 3: Monthly income needed after inflation $7,281

Step 4: Adjusted monthly income needed (step 3 minus other
monthly income) $7,281

Step 5: Size of retirement nest egg at 8% $1,092,150

Step 6:

Step 7:

How Much Money Will You Need to Invest?

Now that we know the size your future nest egg must be, the next and final step is to determine how much money you must put aside to reach that goal. Does this step sound familiar to you? In chapter 2, we established a five-step system to reach a future lump-sum amount. In this case, the lump-sum amount is the size of our nest egg.

There are two sources you may possibly rely upon to get you closer to your goal. The first is any existing account you may already have managed to save. You may have a savings account with your credit union or an IRA account that you opened years ago and just left alone. The second source is the amount of money you will be able to set aside each month between now and retirement time. Obviously, the more money you already have saved the better, since it will mean that you will need a lower monthly amount to invest to reach your desired goal.

Let's assume that you have a credit union account with a balance of $8,000 and a 401(k) at work with a balance of $34,000. That $42,000 can work hard for you between now and retirement. We will use a table similar to the one we used in chapter 2 to project the future value of your existing savings account (that table was the future value of $1, this table is the future value of $1,000). Let's make two assumptions: an 8 percent rate of return in our projections (because you are going to make that money work at least that hard once you are done with this book), and that you are thirty years from retirement.

FUTURE VALUE OF $1,000 INVESTMENT AT VARYING RATES OF RETURN

Years to Goal	Average Annual Interest Earned								
	5%	6%	7%	8%	9%	10%	11%	12%	15%
35	$5,516	$7,686	$10,677	$14,785	$20,414	$28,102	$38,575	$52,800	$133,176
30	$4,322	$5,743	$7,612	$10,063	$13,268	$17,449	$22,892	$29,960	$66,212
25	$3,386	$4,292	$5,427	$6,848	$8,623	$10,835	$13,585	$17,000	$32,919
20	$2,653	$3,207	$3,870	$4,661	$5,604	$6,727	$8,062	$9,646	$16,367
15	$2,079	$2,397	$2,759	$3,172	$3,642	$4,177	$4,785	$5,474	$8,137
10	$1,629	$1,791	$1,967	$2,159	$2,367	$2,594	$2,839	$3,106	$4,046
5	$1,276	$1,338	$1,403	$1,469	$1,539	$1,611	$1,685	$1,762	$2,011

Find thirty years under Years to Goal and move your finger to the right until you find the box under 8 percent. The number there is $10,063. This is how much $1,000 will grow in thirty years at 8 percent. Since we have $42,000, we need to multiply that figure times forty-two.

$$\$10,063 \times 42 = \$422,646$$

This is the value of your $42,000 thirty years from now at 8 percent return per year.

You have just found a significant amount of money that you can apply toward your nest egg without having to add a penny from your pocket. That means that the amount you have to reach with your monthly investments has just been decreased by $422,646. Subtract this amount from your original $1,092,150, and you will get $669,504. This is the adjusted size of your desired nest egg. Let's update our list:

Step 1: Desired monthly income $3,000

Step 2: Years to goal 30

Step 3: Monthly income needed after inflation $7,281

Step 4: Adjusted monthly income needed (step 3 minus other monthly income) $7,281

Step 5: Size of retirement nest egg at 8% $1,092,150

Step 6: Adjusted nest egg size (step 5 minus other accounts) $669,504

Step 7:

Can you guess what the next and final step is? If you answered that you need to figure out how much money you need to set aside on a monthly basis to reach $669,504, you're right!

Let's revisit the Monthly Investment Table we used in the previous chapter to find the answer to that question, assuming an 8 percent return.

MONTHLY INVESTMENT NEEDED TO REACH A $1,000 GOAL

Years to Goal	Average Annual Interest Earned								
	5%	6%	7%	8%	9%	10%	11%	12%	15%
35	.88	.70	.56	.44	.34	.26	.20	.16	.07
30	1.20	1.00	.82	.67	.55	.44	.36	.29	.14
25	1.68	1.44	1.23	1.05	.89	.75	.63	.53	.31
20	2.43	2.16	1.92	1.70	1.50	1.32	1.16	1.01	.67
15	3.74	3.44	3.15	2.89	2.64	2.41	2.20	2.00	1.50
10	6.44	6.10	5.78	5.47	5.17	4.88	4.61	4.35	3.63
5	14.70	14.33	13.97	13.61	13.26	12.91	12.58	12.24	11.29
2	39.70	40.00	39.32	38.94	38.56	38.18	37.81	37.44	36.34

Since you wish to reach your goal in thirty years, find that number under the Years to Goal column. Run your finger to the right until you reach the column under 8 percent. The number there is .67. That figure represents how much money you need to save every month for thirty years at 8 percent to reach $1,000. Since we want to reach $669,504, divide 669,504 by 1,000 then multiply that number by .67. The result will be $448.57.

$$\$669,504 \div 1,000 = \$669.504 \times .67 = \$448.57$$

You will need to set aside $448.57 each month, earning 8 percent, over the next thirty years to achieve your desired nest egg. At that time, you will be able to begin drawing $7,281 each month from that account, which represents 8 percent of your entire amount. This account should last you the rest of your life if you can continue to earn 8 percent. If, once you start taking money out, you earn less interest, we will handle that scenario in chapter 12. Otherwise, your planning and discipline just turned your golden years into your golden age!

You can now fill in the final step in our chart:

Step 1: Desired monthly income $3,000

Step 2: Years to goal 30

Step 3: Monthly income needed after inflation $7,281

Step 4: Adjusted monthly income needed (step 3 minus other monthly income) $7,281

Step 5: Size of retirement nest egg at 8% $1,092,150

Step 6: Adjusted nest egg size (step 5 minus other accounts) $669,504

Step 7: Monthly investment needed to reach goal $448.57

Let's Rewind and Play It Again

These are the steps we took to prepare for a cushy retirement:

STEP 1. Determine how much money you would like to receive on a monthly basis.

STEP 2. Figure out how many years you have until retirement.

STEP 3. Project your future monthly amount after inflation.

STEP 4. Subtract any source of *monthly* income you may have in the future from the amount in step 3.

STEP 5. Use the Nest Egg calculator table on page 42 to find out how much money you will need to accumulate to provide your desired monthly income at retirement.

STEP 6. Project the future value of any existing accounts you may be able to use toward your retirement and subtract that amount from your nest egg amount.

STEP 7. Establish how much money you will need to set aside on a monthly basis to make sure you reach your desired goal.

Financial independence relies on your wisdom to combine three variables: the *amount of money* you have available to invest, the average *annual return* you can get on your money, and the most precious commodity of all: *time*.

You may not have much control over the available amount of money you have toward reaching your financial goals, and we definitely cannot turn back the clock to get more time, but there is one thing we can control, and that is the return we get on our hard-earned money.

Hungry for choices? In the next chapter, we will begin our journey through an investment menu that will satisfy your hunger for profits while keeping you away from the Pepto-Bismol.

CHAPTER FOUR

Investing à la Carte

Remember the first time you went to a Chinese restaurant? Chances are, the list of choices stretched across several pages, each dish more foreign-sounding than the next. After several visits to the restaurant and more than your share of bloopers along the way, you probably settled on a few delicious choices, dishes that perfectly pleased your palate, only tiptoeing into unknown territory when you were really in the mood for adventure.

If choosing the right investment feels like a déjà vu trip to Ming's Restaurant, you will love the coming chapters. Instead of trying out all sorts of strange investments until you find the ones that are right for you, we are going to help you figure out in advance what works for you and what doesn't. You are going to build on what you learned in the previous chapters, morsel by delicious morsel.

You have already figured out how to establish specific financial goals, whether you were saving toward a one-time expense or for a nest egg that would provide future monthly income. Once you determined your desired amount, you followed the steps to figure out the monthly amount it would take to accomplish your goal, given some assumptions of annual interest rates. Those rates of return, estimated at 5 percent and 8 percent, compounded year after year, fueled your account with the power it needed to help you reach your desired destination: a secure financial future.

Now, in this chapter, we will begin to go over your investment menu, and in later chapters I will help you choose the right mutual fund for you, whether you are saving toward a down payment on a car, a summer vacation, a trip around the world, your children's education, or a comfortable and carefree retirement. You will learn how to pick among the overwhelming mutual fund choices available, investing in those that meet not only your return expectations but also your tolerance for risk and your time frame.

What Is Your Estimated Time of Arrival?

Before we can jump right into types of mutual funds, we need to address that crucial issue again: time frame. The most important factor to consider when choosing an investment is to determine *how long* you are willing to wait to cash in your potential profits. And that all depends on when you need access to your money.

The Short-Term Investor

There are two types of short-term goals: short-term goals that you wish to accomplish within the next two years, and short-term goals that you have two to five years to reach. A short-term goal may be to pay off high-interest credit card debt or accumulate enough money for a summer trip or a down payment on a car. Although two years may seem like a long time to wait to attain your goal, in investment-time a two-year period is considered a very short period of time.

When the time that you can invest your money is limited, every penny counts, and the last thing you would want to do is risk all your money in the hopes of making a large profit. Therefore, if you are planning to cash out within two years from now, it would *not* make sense for you to risk your money in the stock market or in mutual funds. If you have two to five years to invest the money, we will cover that later. For now, we're talking short-short term.

The volatility of investing in stocks and mutual funds makes it impossible to predict with any degree of accuracy what the value of your account would be within such a short period of time. Many naive investors, driven by the headlines of extraordinary returns in the market, pour most of their money into individual stocks and mutual funds, only to cash in at the worst possible times: when prices are down and they panic, or when prices are down and they simply need access to their funds.

Although the average annual return of the market has been stellar, remember that it is only an average. Stock investors have suffered temporary (and sometimes not so temporary) setbacks in the market in the past. You must be able to ride out those times when stock prices are low without the added pressure of needing to have instant access to your money.

Take a look at the following chart. It represents the behavior of the U.S. stock market between May 1986 and February 2001. Each vertical bar represents one month. The bars above the horizontal line illustrate

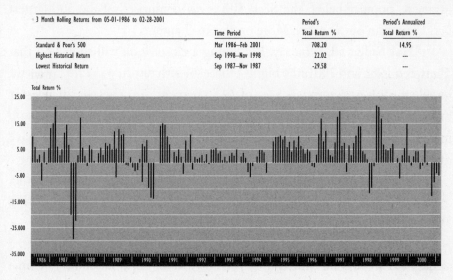

Source: Morningstar®Principia®Pro

the months where stocks increased in value, and the bars below the line are those teeth-clenching months when the value of stocks decreased. The numbers along the left-hand column show the degree of gains or losses with stocks over the years.

The top of the chart shows that the total average return of the S&P 500 Index during that time period was 14.95.

Whoa! What's an index? In investment lingo, an *index* is simply a sampling of different types of companies that make up the entire stock market. Indexes (or indices) break up that huge world of companies into smaller groups of companies that make the stock market easier to analyze.

Without having to ask you to slip into your tweed jacket and light up your pipe, let me explain to you simply that an index is formed by grouping together a set of investments that share similar characteristics. For example, here we're talking about the S&P 500 Index. This index, comprised of— you guessed it: 500 companies—is one of the most closely watched indices in the world. The stocks that make up the S&P 500 are chosen as representatives of the many industries that make up the U.S. economy; it is made up of approximately 400 industrial, 40 utility, 40 financial, and 20 transportation stocks. (Here's a little tip that will let you impress your friends: Contrary to popular belief, the S&P 500 is *not* comprised of the 500 largest companies in our country. More on this in chapter 6.)

"Not bad at all," you say. But taking a closer look will show you that between 1986 and 2001, the highest three-month return was 22.02 percent, while the lowest return was a *loss* of 29.58 percent! Any short-term investor with a time frame of less than two years could have gotten in at the top when they would have had to pay top dollar for various stocks, only to have to sell at the bottom when those stocks were selling for much less. Ouch!

Since it is impossible to anticipate the market correctly all the time, you are better off keeping the money that you are going to need during the next two years out of the race.

So what are your investment choices? If you have set your sights on a goal with a two-year time frame, your investment options should be limited to those that are not subject to the market fluctuations that may decrease the value of your account. However, these options do offer you a lower rate of return. That's the price you have to pay when you cannot afford to risk your money.

Your goal, then, for the next two years is to **save or store** your money in a place where you will not risk losing your *principal* (your initial investment or the money you started out with), but at which you can get a decent rate of return.

Here is a menu of the types of accounts that would offer you the short-term *liquidity* (accessibility to your money) that you need, safety of your principal, and the highest possible returns:

1. *Savings account.* This is the most popular type of account in this category, and most of us are familiar with how one works. You deposit your money and earn interest, which is usually low. Your account is federally insured by the Federal Deposit Insurance Corporation (FDIC) up to $100,000 total per bank. You do not need to commit your money to staying in this account for any specified period of time, so your money is completely liquid, meaning you can withdraw part or all of it at any time. You can open a savings account at almost any bank. Shop around to find out which bank offers the best interest rate.

2. *CD or certificate of deposit.* Banks also offer this type of account. The interest rate you earn is usually higher than what you earn from a regular savings account, but you must commit to not withdrawing your money for a period of time. This period of time may range from one month to ten years. If you consider saving in CDs, don't limit yourself to banks that reside in your state. You can often find higher rates in out-of-state banks. You can go to www.bankrate.com to look for the best CD rates throughout the United States.

In order to choose the best CD for you, first decide how long you are willing to do without access to your money. Is it three months? Six months? Once you determine that, find the best rate for the time frame. You might want to divide your money into two parts and have one three-month CD and one six-month CD. That way, you will have one account maturing every three months while you simultaneously take advantage of a higher return for being willing to commit to a longer period of time. Make sure you always call (800) 934-3342 to verify that the bank you are considering is a member of the FDIC.

3. *T-bills.* Treasury bills are government IOUs. When you buy a T-bill, the government is borrowing money from you and pays you interest on that loan. The full faith and credit of the United States government guarantees that the interest and the original money you invested, the *principal*, will be paid on time. You can buy T-bills from most stockbrokers, who will charge you a commission for opening an account, or you can purchase T-bills directly from the U.S. Treasury Department, at no cost, by contacting TreasuryDirect, P.O. Box 660657, Dallas, TX 75266-0657. Their toll-free phone number is (800) 722-2678. As with a CD, you must be willing to leave your T-bill account untouched for a period of time. The terms for treasury bills are thirteen weeks (three months), twenty-six weeks (six months), or fifty-two weeks (one year). The minimum investment for a T-bill is $1,000. The interest you earn from treasury bills is exempt from state and local income taxes but not from federal taxes.

A T-bill is usually a better candidate for making money than a CD or savings account if you reside in a state that imposes state and local taxes and you are above the federal 28 percent tax bracket.[1]

---

[1] If you don't know your tax bracket and you don't have an accountant to ask, here's how you can find out what your tax bracket is:

Go to www.irs.gov. At the very bottom of the home page, you will see "Tax Info for You"; click there. You will be presented with a table of contents of sorts. Click on "Tax Tables." On that screen, you will see a tax table for the most recent year. There are instructions that read, "Use if your taxable income is less than $100,000. If $100,000 or more, use the Tax Rate Schedules." Regardless of your income (*even if it's less than $100,000*), click on "Tax Rate Schedules." Look for your filing status (are you single; married and filing jointly; etc.?). Once you do this, determine your taxable (your income *minus* your deductions) income range, and the percentage to the right is your tax bracket.

4. *Money market mutual funds and money market accounts.* The last category to consider for your short-term savings is money market accounts.

Money market mutual funds invest in treasury bills and short-term IOUs from corporations with very high credit ratings. A specific example of what they invest in would be a short-term loan to a corporation or large company that comes due in one to ninety days. These types of loans are called *commercial paper loans,* and they are considered relatively safe. Unlike CDs and T-bills, the government does *not* insure this type of account; however, due to the nature of money market mutual funds' investments (they are short term, the companies they invest in are large and stable, and their practices are highly regulated by the government), these types of accounts are considered very safe. Earnings are paid as dividends to shareholders, and investors can write checks against the balance invested in these funds. You do not have to commit to depositing your money for a specific period of time, but some money market mutual funds require a minimum deposit. Money market funds are available directly from mutual fund families (Vanguard, Strong, Fidelity, etc.) or you can go through a brokerage house (such as Schwab, Merrill Lynch, and Olde).

Money market accounts are available from most banks. These accounts are government insured, which may make nervous investors sleep better at night, but historically, their yield is lower. Like a money market mutual fund, you do not have to commit to depositing your money for a set period of time. You have complete access to your money; however, you may have some restrictions regarding the number of withdrawals you may make from your account. Although the average yield may be lower than money market mutual funds, some banks are offering higher yields to attract deposits, so it pays to shop around.

Should you put your money in a money market mutual fund or a money market account? Personally, I tend to favor money market mutual funds. Historically, the returns have been higher, and although these funds are not insured, nobody has ever lost money in a money market mutual fund. However, I encourage you to look at money market mutual funds *and* money market accounts, do some research, and choose what's best for you based on return and your comfort level.

To find the best money market account, follow these steps:

a. Go to www.bankrate.com.

b. Click on the "Select a Product" window and choose "Money Markets."

c. Click the button next to the heading that says: "Select best rate (100 Highest Yields Money Market Accounts)." Click "Go."

d. Now, click on the button that opens the "Select an Account" window and choose the types of money market accounts you are interested in, based on the amount you have to deposit. For lower balances, choose "MMA" (Regular Money Market Account) and click "Go."

e. What you now see is a list of institutions that offer money market accounts, their phone numbers, most recent rates and account particulars, including minimum requirements and possible fees.

To find the best money market mutual fund, follow these steps:

a. Again, go to www.bankrate.com, click on the "Select a Product" window and choose "Money Markets."

b. Now, click on the link that says "Taxable Money Market Mutual Funds" if you want a taxable account, or "Non-taxable Money Market Mutual Funds" if you are in a high tax bracket (28 percent or above) and want to see the rates that are offered in tax-free accounts.

c. You will see a list of institutions and some of the particulars regarding each account.

Regardless of the type of money market you are interested in, make sure you click on the heading of each column for its definition, which will make it easier for you to compare each company at a glance. In a money market acount or mutual fund, it is important to note the minimum amount required for writing a check and how many checks you will be able to write per month with no fees. Make sure you are prepared to abide by these rules before opening your account.

OK, so now that you eliminated some funds, which have the highest yield? That fund seems like a winner, but first you have to check its *prospectus* (a report that tells you all about the fund). To get the fund's prospectus, go on-line to www.sec.gov/edgar/searchedgar/prospectus.htm and in the first open box, type in the name of the fund. (Hint: Don't put in the entire name, just the first word.)

Now don't freak out! Every SEC fund prospectus looks like this, and it is quite overwhelming, but print it out and look over the material. After you do that, I suggest you call the fund directly. You will see a toll-free number on the prospectus. When you call and you tell them you're interested in the fund, the first thing they'll ask you is if you've read the prospectus. Now you can say yes. But you want some answers. Ask if there are any restrictions on the fund. Is there a minimum amount you need to deposit? Are there penalties imposed if you fall below that minimum? Is there a limited amount of checks you can write against the account? And are there any hidden fees? I would also verify the yield, just to make sure the information on the ibcdata web site is correct.

If the answers you receive are satisfactory, you can simply open an account.

Once you have done your homework, you can make an educated decision about what type of money market account is right for you.

Money market accounts may offer you the best place to park your short-term money because of the convenience of having access to your account by writing a check and the freedom of not having to commit to any specific time period.

These four types of accounts should only hold money that you must have access to within two years. Even if you are not saving for a particular cause, it's always wise to keep some money handy in a liquid account earning some interest. Ask yourself the following question: "Am I willing to do without this money for a period longer than two years?" If the answer is no, chances are your money belongs in one of these four types of accounts. If you can keep your hands off the money for two to five years, keep reading. Your strategy will be more like that of a medium- or long-term investor.

The Medium- and Long-Term Investor

What if you are willing to part with your money for a period of two or more years? In that case, can we talk? The rest of this book is designed specifically for you, and you are going to have a feast with the menu that is going to open up before your eyes.

In my previous book, *Get Your Share*, you learned not only how to choose which individual stocks to buy, but also when to buy them and when to sell. We looked at the telltale signs that the market was giving us and acted accordingly to maximize our gains.

While buying individual stocks offers a tremendous opportunity for profit, it requires your undivided attention. The timing of your buys and sells is as important as choosing the right companies to buy. The atmosphere of the market in general and the behavior of individual stocks determines if and when we should be in the market. There are times when the best stock investment is to sit on our cash and wait for the opportunity that is right for us. When you buy stocks, you must keep one eye on your company and the other eye on the atmosphere of the market.

You have to be diligent and pay attention to every hiccup and burp of the stock market in order to succeed in investing in individual stocks. We should date our individual stocks, not marry them, and when we see the writing on the wall that the romance is over, selling is the only solution. *However, these rules apply only to buying and selling <u>individual</u> stocks.*

In this book, we are *not* talking about investing in individual stocks to reach our financial goals. Instead, you are learning how to set your financial plans in motion and leave the day-to-day money managing to someone else; that's what mutual funds are all about! Then you will sit back and spend your time engaged in the activities you enjoy most, while your money works toward your goals for you. The only work you will have to do is monitor your progress.

"Sign me up!" you say. "How can I do that?" By putting your money to work for you in mutual funds, which we will define more in the following chapter.

According to the Securities and Exchange Commission (or SEC), the federal agency that regulates the securities markets, one in three Americans invested in mutual funds in 1999 compared to only one in eighteen in 1980. Why is there all this increased interest in this type of investment? Because investing in mutual funds allows the small investor to participate in the stock market without having to make the day-to-day decisions that are necessary with individual stocks. Public interest in the stock market in general has risen in recent years. But many people have also lost a lot of money investing in individual stocks. That's why investing in mutual funds is like riding in a limousine: You can leave the driving to someone else while you sit back and enjoy the ride!

In the next chapter, I will help you choose the limo company that will take you where you want to go and get you there according to your schedule. Mutual funds, here we come!

CHAPTER FIVE

Your Personal Chauffeur

If you had several million dollars to invest, you would probably hire someone to jump on a plane, go to the headquarters of the companies you were thinking of investing in, barge into the executive offices, dig into their files to do a lot of research, and ask a lot of questions. With that kind of clout, chances are you could also meet with the decision makers of those companies; talk to their employees, bankers, creditors, even their competitors; and walk away with a pretty good idea of whether or not you would want to buy their stock.

As a small investor, you can still afford to have an army of analysts on your team. These analysts will sniff out good investment opportunities and will hire the brains to mastermind buying and selling strategies. How can you get access to this kind of service without already being a millionaire? By joining the growing ranks who are investing in mutual funds.

For as little as twenty-five dollars, you may pool your money along with that of many other investors and have the mutual fund company invest this pool of money on your behalf. Your twenty-five dollars may not buy much, but if that twenty-five dollars goes into a pot of twenty-five million dollars, all that combined money can buy chunks of the best company stocks and can diversify across many different kinds of companies. And that twenty-five million sure has a lot more clout in the financial world, too.

With mutual funds, all you investors *mutually* benefit from the pot of money you all share. You all have the benefits of big stock ownership without having to do all the daily work it takes to research each individual stock, to buy at the right time, and to sell at the right time. With mutual funds, all you investors together hire a manager who does it all for you. More on those guys later, but first, let's dish about the talk on the street.

I Heard It on the Street

There is a term you may have heard bandied about a lot lately: *dollar-cost-averaging*. Have you been dying to know what it really means? Guess what? It's not nearly as exotic as it sounds. Dollar-cost-averaging is simply another way of telling investors to put money aside every month into their investment accounts. Dollar-cost-averaging with mutual funds is simply putting a set amount of money into your mutual fund account every month. Sounds kinda simplistic, doesn't it? That's because it is.

As any seasoned investor knows, there are two ways to invest. The first one is by timing the market; that is, trying to pinpoint the exact time when it might be more beneficial to invest and refraining from doing so when the conditions are not favorable. In *Get Your Share*, we learned that when you buy individual stocks, it is imperative that you be able to time your purchases during a period when the market in general is in an *uptrend* (which means going up, a *bull* market), but you must also be able to tell by reading the technical charts when your particular individual stock gives you the signal that it is time to buy.

The second method of investing is that in which you deposit into your account the same amount of money, at regular intervals, regardless of what the market in general or your investment in particular is doing. For instance, you deposit $100 every month into your investment account in order to reach a lump-sum, medium-term goal such as a college fund or $300 every month in order to reach a long-term retirement goal. This is what is called dollar-cost-averaging. As you have seen in chapters 2 and 3 when you figured out how much you needed to put aside monthly to reach your goals, successful mutual fund investing calls for this steady method of regular deposits.

The reason that you benefit from dollar-cost-averaging is that your money, going into the fund at a steady pace, will end up buying more shares when the price is down and fewer shares when the price is up, ending up with an *average* share price. How does this happen? Studies have shown that the average share price achieved by dollar-cost-averaging is, in most cases, lower than the average share price achieved by investors who try to time their mutual fund purchases thinking that they can anticipate the precise, perfect moment to purchase. Maybe fund managers actually do earn their pudding after all!

Dollar-cost-averaging is a no-brainer method of acting smart. It's nice to know that by doing something by rote, you are really making the most intelligent decision, leaving the baby-sitting up to the mutual fund's baby-sitters. Huh? A mutual fund has baby-sitters?

Mutual Fund Managers: The Ultimate Baby-sitters

Each mutual fund has a manager or group of managers whose job it is to baby-sit your money. They use the money in the fund's pot to buy and sell stocks, bonds, or a combination of the two on our behalf. These managers make it their business to know the companies that they buy inside out, often taking trips to company headquarters to check out things firsthand and talking to customers, bankers—the works. There are also analysts who are hired to assist the fund managers in studying market trends and evaluating up-and-coming new products and services that may affect the value of the holdings of the mutual funds. They take their job very seriously. A lot of money is riding on their decisions.

The managers of a fund usually meet every day and decide how to adjust their holdings to maintain or increase their profits and to keep their shareholders happy. And, just as parents are happiest when their babies are well cared for, shareholders are happiest when they're making money.

It's a Family Affair

Mutual funds come in *families*. You may have heard of Franklin Mutual Funds, Vanguard, Fidelity, Oppenheimer—all of these are fund families. These families of funds may have one or many offspring, called *individual funds*.

For example, the Vanguard mutual fund family has over fifty individual mutual funds under its name, each one with unique characteristics. Some of these offspring are very aggressive funds, investing in newer companies that may be at the cutting edge of technology. Some are passive, concentrating on well-established companies that have had a slow, steady growth over the years. And some are in between, combining characteristics of the two previous choices.

So How Does It Work?

When you buy shares of a mutual fund, you are buying shares in the fund itself, and in turn, that fund buys and sells stocks, bonds, or a combination of the two, with your money. The value of the shares you own will go up or down depending on the value of each of the individual stocks or bonds the fund owns.

After the market closes, your mutual fund company adds up the closing price of all the *securities* (a fancy term for stocks, bonds, or other investments) that it owns and divides its total value by the number of shares it has issued to investors like us. The end result is called the NAV or *Net Asset Value* of that fund. To remember what the NAV is, write down this definition in your notebook: *NAV = total closing price of all stocks and bonds in fund ÷ shares issued to investors.*

This number, the NAV, is available to us each day in the business section of our daily newspaper, on the Internet, or by calling the mutual fund company directly. When you request the NAV for a fund, you will be given the price for the last closing day. Mutual fund shares, unlike stock prices, are calculated only once a day, at closing time. Closing time of the market is 4:00 P.M. eastern standard time, when the stock market closes its doors. That's when mutual fund share prices are determined.

You never know exactly how much money you will pay for your share, since the mutual fund company must receive your money first. Once they receive your check, you will be buying at the price per share as of the following closing.

For example, if a fund receives your money on Tuesday morning, you will buy its shares at the closing price that Tuesday afternoon when the market closes. When you want to sell your shares, say the following Friday, your request to sell will be processed by the fund company at that following Friday's closing price as well. You will sell your shares at that following Friday's NAV.

Some funds also add fees to the price of each share. This is one of the ways the fund makes money to pay its managers and other costs it incurs. We will talk about these sales charges or *loads* in chapter 7.

Every time you buy or sell shares of a mutual fund, you will receive a confirmation of your purchase with the amount deposited by you, the price per share you paid, and the number of shares you purchased. Write down in your notebook how many shares you own, because you can find out how much money your account is worth at any time by multiplying the fund's NAV price published in the paper times the number of shares you have in the fund.

How Exactly Do I Make Money in Mutual Funds?

Even though you are reading this book, I know you aren't here just to hang out and shoot the breeze with me. What you really want to know is what's in it for you. How do you make money or *profits* in a mutual fund? There are three ways:

1. *By receiving dividends (or interest).* You may have chosen a mutual fund company that pays dividends. When that mutual fund receives the dividends from their holdings, they must pass the dividends on to their stockholders. You may wish to receive these dividends in the form of a check or you may have the fund buy more shares with your dividend payments and add them into your account. Even though you are given this choice when you apply for a mutual fund account, you may change your mind and notify the fund of your decision at any time. Because of compound interest, your account will grow faster if you reinvest the dividends back into your fund.

2. *By receiving capital gains.* The mutual fund manager will buy and sell stocks and bonds, hoping to make a profit. Whether the sale results in a profit or a loss, they must pass that profit or loss on to you, the shareholder. You may choose to receive capital gains (read: cash profits) when distributed by the fund or choose to buy additional shares with your capital gains distribution. As with dividend payments, you may change how you wish to receive your capital gains at any time. Reinvesting your capital gains is a good way to add some fuel to your account without having to take money out of your pocket to buy additional shares.

3. *By selling your shares once the share price goes up.* You may sell some or all of the shares you own in a fund. You will sell at the fund's NAV price after they receive your request to sell. You may notify the fund by telephone in many cases or you can send them a written request. By law, the mutual fund company must send you a check within seven days from the date of sale. You may wish to *redeem* (sell) a specific number of shares, or you may not know how many shares you want to sell but wish to receive a specific dollar amount. Either order to sell is acceptable to a mutual fund. A statement confirming your sale will be generated and sent to you with the number of shares sold, the dollar amount sent to you, and the share balance remaining in your account.

Where Can I Buy Shares of a Mutual Fund?

Buying shares of a fund is easier than opening a credit card account. Really! The fund company will give you a copy of their *prospectus* (a very important document that tells you in detail all about the company), their most recent annual report (where they show the fund's recent investment results), and a new account application.

You can open a mutual fund account by calling the company direct on their toll-free number, by going through a stockbroker or financial planner, or by using the Internet. Even banks can sell mutual funds. I do not recommend that you buy a mutual fund from a bank, however. Usually, banks will have an agreement with one or two mutual fund companies and your choice of investments will be limited to theirs. Wouldn't you rather have access to the entire universe of funds than to be given a very limited number of choices? Buy mutual funds either directly from the funds or through your personal financial advisor.

If you like punching the keys on your own keyboard, you can download and print the particular fund's prospectus and the application from your PC. All you would then need to do is write a check to the fund and mail it all in. Regardless of how you choose to open your account, you must wait for a confirmation from the mutual fund to find out how many shares you own and the price you paid for each share.

With a Manager to Watch Over Me

Now that you know a little about the ins and outs of mutual funds, we can start talking about some specifics. Most mutual funds are carefully watched over by managers who buy and sell on your behalf in order to make a profit and pass this profit on to you. These funds, called *managed funds*, are managed on a daily basis by the decision makers of the fund actively moving in and out of stocks or bonds on your behalf.

There are four main kinds of managed mutual funds:

1. *Money market mutual funds*. This type of mutual fund has a relatively low risk compared to other mutual funds. This type of fund is limited by law to invest in high-quality, short-term investments. Money market mutual funds are used primarily as a place to keep money for a relatively short period of time. We discussed money market mutual funds in chapter 4.

2. *Bond funds* (*also called* fixed income funds). When a mutual fund company invests in a bond, it is lending money to a government body or to a corporation and receiving interest payments in the interim. The expiration date of the loan and the credit rating of the company to whom the fund has lent its money can vary, and with it, the potential risk assumed by the investor. We will go over bond funds in detail in chapter 10.

3. *Stock funds* (*also called* equity funds). These are funds that are invested in shares of stock of corporations. Their fate is directly tied to that of the company in which they are invested. A mutual fund company invests in a company's stock with the hope of selling those shares sometime in the future at a higher price than what they paid for them. Not all stock funds are the same. Within this category a mutual fund may concentrate on small, medium, or large companies; it may invest in stocks of a particular sector, such as technology, for example; or it may buy stocks of well-established companies.

4. *Hybrid funds* (*also known as* moderate allocation *or* balanced funds). This type of mutual fund buys a combination of stocks and bonds.

We will look at stock, bond, and hybrid mutual funds in the coming chapters.

Going on Autopilot with Index Funds: The Mutual Funds *Without Active* Managers

Not all mutual funds have active managers to watch over them. You also have at your disposal some one-stop choices that put your investments on cruise control. These funds operate differently from managed funds because they invest in the stocks or bonds that make up the market's indexes, and then they passively wait to make a profit. (Remember that we defined indexes on page 52.)

These mutual funds without managers that are based on indices are called, you guessed it, *index funds*. These types of funds are perfect for those of you who are looking for a way to go on mutual fund autopilot and not have to read the rest of this book.

Probably the most popular index fund is the Vanguard Index 500. This index mutual fund, as the name implies, buys the 500 stocks that make up the Standard & Poor's 500 Index. Then, like the Maytag repairman in the commercials, your money just sits in the investment and waits. There are no managers, so there's no buying and selling. The money just waits there to grow.

The only time that an index fund sells and buys new securities is when the index itself makes a change in one of its members. For example, two companies that are part of an index may merge, leaving a vacancy. A new company is brought in to fill that vacancy, and any mutual fund company that has an index fund based on that index must make the adjustment as well by substituting one company with the other in their holdings.

The main advantage of an index fund is that the costs related to its management are low. Since there is very little activity in the holdings of the fund, the fund's costs are low and therefore savings are passed on to the investors of the fund. You can keep track of how your index fund is doing by following the index itself, without having to rely on your specific mutual fund reports or even your quarterly statements. Also there are usually less capital gains taxes generated by index funds since there is less buying and selling going on.

The main disadvantage of an index fund is that you can only hope to do as well as the index that your fund represents—and it's a big pool. When the index goes down, your fund goes down, and you are not protected by the manager's ability to keep more of the fund's money in cash or her ability to buy and sell to keep the profits up.

S&P 500 Index funds have had a tremendous popularity. By investing in this type of mutual fund, you are spreading your money among the stocks that are considered representative of the market in general. Studies have also shown that most managed funds have not outperformed the S&P 500 Index on a regular basis. This plain vanilla investment is one of the most popular choices of mutual fund investors. If you are interested in a stock mutual fund and you are willing to put the time and effort into finding one with a better record than the S&P 500 Index funds, your efforts will pay off. If, however, you wish to be in the stock market but do not want to attempt to beat its average return, then this no-brainer mutual fund may be right for you.

A Star Is Born

If S&P 500 Index funds were the talk of the town in recent years, the year 2000 saw the dawning of a new breed of investment choices: the index-based *Exchange-Traded Funds*, referred to in the investment world as ETFs.

An ETF is a mutual fund that trades like a single stock. It is a basket of stocks that reflects the composition of an index, just like index funds, the only difference being that instead of a normal mutual fund that determines its NAV (Net Asset Value) price at the end of each trading day, an ETF is bought and sold in real time, just like an individual stock, so its share price changes throughout the day.

The benefit of using ETFs is that you, as an investor, can enjoy the flexibility of a stock and the diversification of an index fund at the same time. The expenses of an ETF are even lower than that of an index fund.

As an investor in ETFs, however, you incur some expenses that are unique to this type of investment. Since they are bought and sold as shares through a broker, every time an investor makes a purchase, he pays a commission to his broker of eight dollars and up, depending on the broker.

You may have also overheard someone on your way to work talking about *spiders*. They are not discussing a pest problem. A SPDR (which stands for Standard & Poor's Depository Receipts) is the first U.S.-based ETF that opened in 1993. It invests in the stocks that make up the S&P 500 Index.

ETFs are currently trading on the American Stock Exchange, though the New York Stock Exchange is planning to introduce these investments in the near future. Shares can be purchased in the same way you would buy an individual stock: through most stockbrokers.

The popularity of ETFs has earned them a place on Morningstar.com, where you can find additional information regarding this type of investment. Morningstar, Inc. is a company that serves as an independent reporting authority on mutual funds, much like *Consumer Reports* does for consumer products. Lipper, Inc. is another highly respected reporting company. Both can be accessed on-line. As the popularity of ETFs continues to grow, you will probably hear a lot more about them in the years to come. However, even though this investment is similar to an index fund in that it holds a basket of stocks that make up an index, ETFs carry additional features that affect the price of their shares.

I consider ETFs middle ground between mutual funds and individual stocks, so if you are new to investing in general, skip on this choice until you feel you have mastered the process of choosing a quality mutual fund.

Open-end and Closed-end Mutual Funds

I know you're just ready to jump in and invest now that you know about some of the kinds of mutual funds. But there's just a bit more to go over before we can do that. All of the kinds of mutual funds you just learned about fall into one of two categories: *open-end* or *closed-end* funds. An *open-end* mutual fund is one that accepts money from new investors all the time.

When you invest in an open-end mutual fund, you do so with the knowledge that at any time you wish to sell your shares and get some cash, the company itself will buy them back from you at the current price of each share. In other words, an open-end mutual fund company has a return policy (but remember that you will get back an amount of money reflecting the new share price, not the price you paid for your share when you bought it).

A *closed-end* fund acts more like a stock than a traditional mutual fund. If you wish to sell closed-end fund shares, you cannot do so with the fund company. They do not pay money back. Instead, to sell and get some cash, you have to find another investor who is willing to buy your shares at the current price.

In an open-end fund, investors can put money in and take money out of the fund. In a closed-end fund, investors buy and sell the shares of the fund to other investors in the market.

We will concentrate on open-end mutual funds, since one in every three households has an open-end mutual fund.

What's the Real Scoop?

OK, so you are getting more and more familiar with this world of mutual funds and are ready to hop in that limo and get going. But not so fast. Rats! Wouldn't you know it? Every pretty box comes with a warning label, and here is ours. Once you do all the research on a fund on-line or at the library, how can you be sure that what you've read about the fund is accurate?

For starters, you should know that the mutual fund world is regulated by the government, thanks to changes that have taken place after the Crash of 1929, when so many individual investors lost their money in closed-end funds.

The U.S. Securities and Exchange Commission (SEC) is the federal agency that protects the individual investor by regulating the disclosure by mutual fund companies of important information that we investors need to have in order to be able to make intelligent decisions in choosing a mutual fund company.

As part of the requirements of the SEC, every mutual fund company must publish and abide by a document I mentioned earlier called a *prospectus*, which describes—in language void of adjectives that might be construed as sales tools—the main characteristics of each of their funds. The prospectus (a document many of my clients have referred to as "that Greek-sounding thing") must be presented to an investor prior to the sale of any mutual fund. In it, you will find the goal of the fund, its fees and expenses, its investment strategies, the risks of the fund, and the minimum investment requirement, as well as how to buy and sell its shares. All mutual fund companies have to file their prospectuses with the SEC. While we will talk more about prospectuses later and the information that you will look for in them, you can view these prospectuses for almost any given mutual fund at www.sec.gov/edgar/searchedgar/prospectus.htm.

The SEC does not make any guarantees on the return you might receive from any investment. All they concern themselves with is that each mutual fund company discloses the same information to any person interested in making an investment in any of their funds. *Any money you invest in a mutual fund company is not guaranteed or insured by any public or private organization.* This is a very important factor to keep in mind, especially for those of you who invest in mutual funds through your local bank. *Mutual funds you purchase from your bank are not insured. The value of your account, including the money that you deposited, could go up or down.*

That said, one of the reasons mutual funds are so popular is that the SEC also mandates that mutual funds invest in many securities to minimize risk. When one security drops, chances are another security in the fund is making money, and the two balance each other out. There is a smaller likelihood that all the investments in a mutual fund will drop at the same time.

Enough Yapping, Let's Get on with the Show!

Now that you have an idea of how mutual funds work, the next step is to learn how to choose a mutual fund that will take you closer to your financial goals.

We will concentrate on those mutual funds that have proven most profitable in the past on a *consistent* basis. There are lots of other types of mutual funds that you may have heard of. In fact, there are funds upon funds that crowd the financial pages of newspapers. Many of them offer short-term gains but fall short of consistent and stable returns. For your long-term needs, we are going to stick with tried-and-true basics. You're in it for steady profit, not entertainment.

As my old Cuban grandma used to say when talking about prospective husbands, you may like a little hot sauce on your steak, but you would never consider making an entire meal out of it. We will concentrate on a well-balanced mutual fund meal with just the right blend of protein, carbohydrates, and fat to keep your system running smoothly. We are not interested in junk food when we are talking about our financial future.

In the next chapter, I will show you how to find a fund that satisfies your appetite for success.

CHAPTER SIX

Targeting the Best Mutual Fund for You

On September 20, 1998, Cal Ripken played his 2,632nd consecutive game, the longest continuous streak of games in the history of baseball. How did this baseball player become a legend? By performing well, consistently, over time. Mutual funds can also become legendary in the financial world by consistently delivering strong returns over time.

But even though mutual funds can be great performers, they aren't for everyone. They are not insured, so, unlike with a savings account at a bank, you can lose your money. They are not for short-term investors of two years or less, because they can be volatile. So if you followed the steps we covered in previous chapters in which we projected your future goals and saw that a 4 percent or 5 percent return on your money would be enough to get you where you want to go, there is no need for you to go any further. Keep your money in a savings account, CD, T-bill, or money market account/money market mutual fund. You can find out information about the best rates out there in those four choices by checking out www.bankrate.com.

If, however, your investment goal requires a higher return on your money than that offered by the "safe" investments I just mentioned, you need to familiarize yourself with the few tools in this chapter that will help you separate the players from the wanna-bes and concentrate on those funds that may get you where you want to go in the fastest, safest possible way.

Even better, you will get to use an easy-to-understand system to choose the best fund for *you*. And what makes a fund the best fund for you is that the fund manager invests the money you have entrusted to him/her in the same manner *you* would have done, within the parameters of your personal financial goals, had you had the same time, knowledge, and experience.

"Great, marvelous, fabulous," you say. "But how on earth am I supposed to choose from among the over 12,300 mutual funds out there?" Indeed, how do you discover the real players in the mutual fund industry? The same way that a sports team manager chooses which players to offer those monster-sized contracts: again, *by looking at how the player has performed, consistently, over time.*

"OK," you say. "I've been paying attention so far. I now know what my financial goals are, and I know I need to make more than 4 percent or 5 percent on my money. I also know that I don't want to baby-sit every stock I choose, so I am going to let a mutual fund manager do that for me with a fund that has performed well consistently over time. But how do I understand *what* exactly consistent performance *is?*"

That's what this chapter is all about. I am going to walk you through the process of choosing the mutual fund that is right for *you*. Then we are going to figure out, together, what exactly consistent performance looks like.

And to do all that, we are first going to use the process of elimination. The first part of my system involves using this handy target for organizing the criteria we will use for making a decision. Here's the target (which you can print out at www.JulieStav.com).

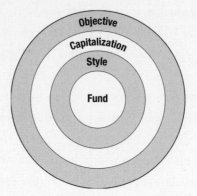

And in order to fill in the rings of this target, we are going to use Aunt Mary's story to illustrate the process.

Bull's-eye for Aunt Mary

Those of us who live life to the fullest plan new goals all the time. On her seventy-third birthday, Aunt Mary announced to her room of friends and well-wishers that her newest dream involved a cruise on the *QE2* with a certain retired gentleman friend before she reached the age of eighty. So, with energy to spare, our feisty femme fatale set out to map her course.

To do this trip right, Aunt Mary figured out that she needs $15,000 in seven years. She has heard about the average returns of the stock market and figures that she could safely aim toward a 10 percent return on her money. Using our five-step chart, she determines that she needs to set aside $123 a month toward her goal.

So Aunt Mary sets out to find the perfect mutual fund for her.

Get Ready . . . for Criterion #1: Growth or Income?

There are 12,300 mutual funds out there, all wishing they had access to your hard-earned money. So how do you start to eliminate some of them? You need to first look at three criteria that apply to all funds and then match those criteria to your financial goals.

In looking at this first criterion, the outer ring of our target, the question we need to ask ourselves is whether we are investing for *growth*—meaning that we want to accumulate money to use sometime in the future—or *income*—which means that we want to generate money from our investment right away.

Fund managers refer to this first criterion (growth or income) as the fund's *objective*. A fund objective is one of the most important factors to consider when making an investment choice, since that manager or group of managers must stay true to the investment objective to which they have committed themselves. If they have committed to being a growth fund, then they must make choices that make growth happen. The SEC, which oversees all mutual funds, requires that every fund include their objective in the fund's prospectus.

Growth means stocks. If the fund manager invests in stocks, it is his or her hope *to cash in those shares at a higher price sometime in the future.* Other words you will find to describe a growth objective are *equity* or *capital appreciation.* When you see these terms, they are telling you that these mutual funds are banking on the future value of their accounts and are not interested in providing income from their investments today.

A fund may also invest for income. *Income means money now, not later.* These are funds that may invest in either bonds (because bonds pay interest) or in shares of companies that pay *dividends* (a portion of a company's earnings that it pays to its shareholders).

Simply said, the objective of a fund will tell you whether the purpose of the mutual fund is to invest for *growth* or for *income*.

Later in this book I will show you how to go on-line to find and evaluate funds grouped by their objective. If, however, you have already done your eliminating and you want to look at the objective of a particular fund on-line, go to www.sec.gov/edgar/searchedgar/prospectus.htm and you will be able to find your fund's prospectus.[1]

---

[1] To find a prospectus on the SEC site, enter the link above, and you will get to the information page. In the first open box, type in the name of the fund. (Hint: Don't type in the entire name, just the first word.) Now, don't be scared. Every SEC fund prospectus looks like this on-line, so all you have to do is start scrolling down the screen until you hit in capital letters: FUND OBJECTIVE. There it is!

"What does a growth or income objective look like when it appears in a prospectus?" you might ask. The following quotes are lifted directly from various mutual fund prospectuses:

"*. . . The fund seeks to provide long-term capital growth. . . .*" (growth fund).

"*. . . The fund seeks to provide the maximum dividend income. . . .*" (income fund).

"*. . . The fund seeks to provide long-term capital growth and income. . . .*" (growth and income fund).

"*The fund seeks to provide a high and sustainable level of income along with moderate long-term capital growth. . . .*" (growth and income fund).

Your next question might be, "How have funds with different objectives performed in general?" Take a look at the following chart that shows the average yearly growth of mutual funds that have different objectives. The government bond and the corporate bond funds are income funds.

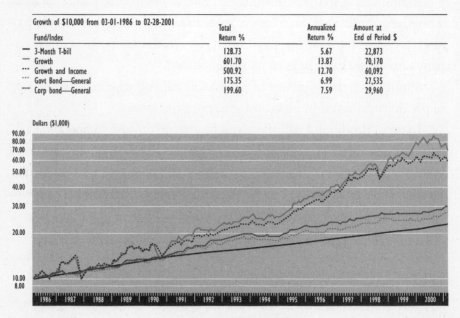

Growth of $10,000 from 03-01-1986 to 02-28-2001 Fund/Index	Total Return %	Annualized Return %	Amount at End of Period $
— 3-Month T-bill	128.73	5.67	22,873
··· Growth	601.70	13.87	70,170
··· Growth and Income	500.92	12.70	60,092
··· Govt Bond—General	175.35	6.99	27,535
— Corp bond—General	199.60	7.59	29,960

Source: Morningstar®Principia®Pro

Compare their average returns with those of growth funds and combined growth and income funds. This chart also shows what a ninety-day T-bill returned during the same time period.

As you can see, funds with *growth* objectives had an average yearly return of 13.87 percent. *Growth and Income* funds—those that invested in stocks that paid dividends—showed a return of 12.70 percent, and *government* and *corporate* bond funds trailed behind with 6.99 percent and 7.59 percent respectively. They all outperformed the average yearly return of 5.67 percent of a ninety-day treasury bill during the illustrated time period. That means that in today's market, funds with a growth objective usually yield the highest return.

Aunt Mary, knowing that her timeline places her goal at seven years from now, feels it makes sense to aim high, so she opts to invest in growth funds. After all, she doesn't need the money now; she'll need the money for her trip in seven years. Aunt Mary takes her target and fills in the objective ring with the word *growth*.

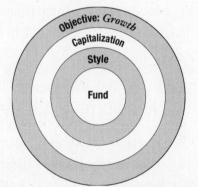

What is your objective? This question might be an easy one for you to answer. *It depends on how long until you need to start spending your investment money.*

If your goal is to buy a new car in two years, forget objectives; you are a short-term investor, and you need to park your money in one of the safe places we discussed in chapter 4.

If you are saving toward a college fund in fifteen years (a medium- to long-term goal, depending on the ages of your children), you don't need to receive any profits from it right now, so your objective is growth; keep reading.

If you are thirty-five years old and working on your nest egg retirement account, your objective is also growth; keep reading some more.

If you just hit the lottery, don't want to work anymore, and want to live off your booty's interest, your objective is getting some income now, which we'll discuss more in chapter 10.

If you want to pay off your credit card debt in three, four, or five years, your objective is mixed, so keep reading but make no decisions until you read chapter 10.

Whatever your objective is, figure it out, and fill in the outermost ring of your target.[2]

As Aunt Mary's objective makes her a growth investor, she has just eliminated all funds that are not growth funds. As she gets closer to her goal in four or five years, she may shift into income funds. But for now, since she is at the beginning of her financial journey and her focus is in making her investment grow, not generating current income. Let's continue. We have just eliminated 4,000 funds; 8,300 to go!

Get Set . . . for Criterion #2:
Small, Medium, or Large?

A fund manager has the option of investing in large, medium, or small companies. But how do you measure the size of a company? By its square footage? No, by its capitalization, the next ring in the target. Stay with me here.

In order to calculate the size of a company, you multiply the number of shares it has offered to the public times the value of each share. For

---

[2] If you still aren't sure about what your objective is, mark this page and skip ahead to the chart in chapter 11 on page 179 in the section entitled "How to Stuff Your Investment Drawers." There you will see how to allocate your money if you are within five years of your goal. Then come back and read on!

example, if a company has 300 million shares, and the stock trades at $50 per share, bingo, that company is worth $15 billion.

$$300 \text{ million shares} \times \$50 = \$15 \text{ billion}$$

Large-capitalization or *large-cap* companies are those that are worth $10 billion or more. Some large-cap companies you probably recognize are Ford Motor Company and McDonald's. Medium-sized firms are called mid-capitalization firms or simply *mid-caps*. These are businesses worth between $1.5 billion and $10 billion. Companies like Intuit (the creator of Quicken software) form part of this group. Finally, *small-cap* companies are valued at $1.5 billion or less. These are smaller companies like Gadzooks, Inc., a specialty retailer of casual apparel for young people.

It would be very difficult to keep track of every company within a size category, so one of the best ways to identify what investors are favoring now is to take a look at a small sample of stocks that represent large-, medium-, or small-cap funds. In investment lingo, this sampling is called an *index*.

You learned about indexes in chapter 4, when we talked about the S&P 500. We have indexes that represent the Goliaths of the stock market as well as the Davids. In fact, there are dozens of indexes, each one representing just about any stock grouping you may think of.

According to traditional belief, mutual funds that invest in smaller companies have a higher potential for gains than their more mature cousins, the large- or mid-cap firms. But a look at historical returns over the past ten years has proven that it doesn't pay to generalize in the stock market, and that as informed investors, we need to redirect our investment money based on what investors are favoring, not on overgeneralizations that may no longer hold true.

Take a look at a chart that illustrates the growth of large-, medium-, and small-cap stocks over the years as represented by their respective indexes.

**LISTING OF AVERAGE YEARLY RETURNS FOR
LARGE-, MID-, AND SMALL-CAP INDICES AS OF 11-30-03**

Index Name	Category	1-Yr Return	3-Yr Return	5-Yr Return	10-Yr Return
S&P 100	Large Cap	10.88%	−16.43%	0.64%	N/A
S&P Mid Cap 400	Mid Cap	27.87%	−0.06%	6.40%	11.95%
S&P Small Cap 600	Small Cap	31.76%	0.56%	2.44%	9.71%
3-Mo. T-bill	Fixed Income	1.08%	3.87%	4.3%	4.54%

Source: www.indexfunds.com

So much for traditional wisdom! As Aunt Mary can see by the chart above, at the time this book was printed, mid-cap companies have taken and held the lead for the past ten years. So in today's market, she figures that mid-cap companies seem like the way to go. Aunt Mary has just reduced her mutual fund pool from 8,300 funds to 1,005 by making the choice to find the best fund within the mid-cap group!

What is your capitalization choice? You may go to www.index-funds.com[3] to help you gauge how the market trend favors each company-

---

[3] Go to www.indexfunds.com. On the home page, scroll down to "Data Central." In the drop-down window, choose "Indexes." Hit the "GO" button. You will see some titles with boxes next to them. Check off "Large Cap," "Mid Cap," and "Small Cap." Then, above these boxes, you will see a drop-down window next to "Sort by"; in that window choose "3-Year Returns." Now go down to the "Screen" button and hit it. A list of indexes appears. Take a look at the top five rows of indexes and count how many times you see the words *Large Cap*, *Mid Cap*, or *Small Cap*. Whichever word appears most gets your vote.

size index. Knowing who has the current lead will help you in narrowing down your investment choices later, so mark it in your notebook. For now, fill in the capitalization ring of your target with your answer.

Go! . . . for Criterion #3: Investment Styles

The third ring in the target is investment style. There are different styles of investing in the market. Some investors look for stocks that are value priced. Others look for stocks that are higher priced but have a lot of growth potential. Still others look for a mix.

In *Get Your Share*, we concentrated on the individual stocks that had demonstrated they had what it took to get ahead, and we bought when their price was within 10 percent of the highest price they had shown during the past year. Bottom-fishing for value stocks was not for us, because we knew that in the stock market, an individual stock was generally priced to go for just about what it was worth. History has shown that once an individual stock hits a new price it tends to continue on this trend and make a higher high. In keeping with this aggressive style, when we invested in individual stocks, there was a time to be in and a time to be out of the market.

In mutual funds, however, the rules are not the same.

So if you are a reader of *Get Your Share*, don't feel you are being fickle if you use a different strategy to identify which mutual funds are making money in the market. That said, there are three types of investment styles that a fund manager may adopt when buying stocks.

The first style is called *value investing*. A value investment manager is the type of fund manager who likes to buy stocks that are selling for what he/she may consider bargain prices. Perhaps the manager is willing to wait until a company with tremendous potential can begin to show profits, even though they are not in positive territory at the moment. These shoppers of out-of-favor stocks usually have a buy-and-hold philosophy.

The second style of manager is one who doesn't mind paying more for a stock as long as it has the winning characteristics that he/she pursues, such as earnings. These *growth investment* managers are willing to take a chance in the stock of a company that they feel has what it takes to increase its earnings over time and eventually leave the competition in the dust. (Note that the word *growth* here, as in *growth investment*, refers to a company's earnings, while a *growth objective* in criterion #1 refers to a mutual fund that invests in stocks. I am convinced, and so is Aunt Mary, that this is yet another example of the investment world's plot to confuse regular people like you and me.)

The third investment style is called a *blend*, and, just as it sounds, it is a mixture of the two styles we mentioned above. The manager may invest in some out-of-favor stocks while keeping some of the fund's money in up-and-coming leaders that have already shown great promise for growth.

Why do you need to know this? Because market cycles favor different investment styles in mutual funds at different times. Because of changes in market cycles, you may later alter some of the investment decisions you make today. For example, for much of the 1990s, growth stocks, particularly technology, dominated the investment arena. But the year 2000 brought about an abrupt change: As the technology bubble burst, value stocks began to soar, and by September 2000, growth indexes were showing a loss of 1.6 percent for the year while value stocks were up by 4.1 percent as reflected in the value indexes.

Growth stocks tend to do well when the stock market as a whole is rising. Value stocks tend to shine when the stock market is falling or just treading water.

"How do I recognize what an investment style looks like in a prospectus or in an on-line mutual fund report?" asks Aunt Mary.

To find that information on the Internet you can go to the mutual funds Morningstar Quicktake® Report on www.morningstar.com.[4] There are two places in the report that indicate investment style. The first is entitled "Data Interpreter." It gives a clear idea of how aggressive

---

[4] To find investment style information on a fund, go to www.morningstar.com. On their home page you will see a box that asks you to "Enter ticker or name." There you will type in the name of the fund and then hit the gray "GO!" button. What appears on the screen will be a mutual fund Quicktake® Report. Click on the "Data Interpreter" button on the navigational bar at the left of your screen.

this manager is in his/her investment approach. Here is an example from an actual on-line mutual fund Morningstar Quicktake® Report:

Inside Scoop

This fund has an especially strong bent toward growth stocks, even compared with other funds that focus on this part of the market. Growth stocks can have considerable upside potential, but they often trade at high prices. If they don't deliver the rapid growth expected of them, they can fall sharply. These stocks can be quite volatile. This fund's average market cap is much lower than even most funds with a small-growth style.

Source: www.morningstar.com

The words "can fall sharply" and "quite volatile" indicate that this is not a buy-and-hold value investment. This fund clearly favors growth investment.

The second area in the Quicktake® Report that indicates investment style is the Morningstar® Style Box™. It resembles the tic-tac-toe game we used to play when we were little. In Morningstar's Quicktake® Reports, these boxes are referred to as a mutual fund's "investment valuation." It's pretty easy to figure out how it works: We have three market caps: small-, medium-, and large-caps, and three investment styles: growth, value, and blend. Three times three equals nine. Right? There are nine possible combinations from which to choose. This is what a Style Box looks like on-line. Can you tell what type of companies these funds invest in? Give it a try.

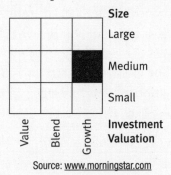

Source: www.morningstar.com

This mutual fund invests in medium-sized companies, and the manager uses a growth approach, buying stocks in companies whose earnings are expected to grow at a fast rate.

Here is another valuation box. What is the investment style of this fund?

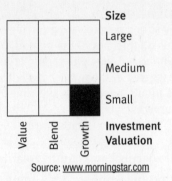

Source: www.morningstar.com

Did you take a shot at guessing? This Style Box shows a mutual fund that invests in small-cap companies, and the manager has a growth approach to picking stocks.

To get all this information on your own, all you have to do is follow the steps we outlined here. You can use the Net to get prospectuses, to run searches on indexes, and to determine market trends.

But back to Aunt Mary. Here she is. She knows you can find this on-line information in the hard copy Morningstar report at the library, but she's still not sure which investment style to choose. To help her out, we are going to look at some recent history. I got this graph from www.indexfunds.com.[5] It shows the difference in return between value and growth mid-caps in the past ten years. Here's what I got:

Index Name	1-Yr Return	3-Yr Return	5-Yr Return	10-Yr Return
Barra Mid Cap Growth	25.41%	–6.71%	7.11%	11.34%
Barra Mid Cap Value	30.31%	7.18%	5.69%	12.33%

Source: www.indexfunds.com

[5] Go to www.indexfunds.com. On the home page, scroll down to "Data Central." In the drop-down window, choose "Indexes." Hit the "GO" button. Check off the boxes for "Mid-Cap" (or whatever your capitalization choice), "Growth," and "Value." Then up above all the boxes, choose "3-Yr Returns" from the drop-down window next to "Sort by." Scroll down and hit "Screen."

These Barra indexes show that value funds have enjoyed a great advantage in the past twelve months as illustrated by the one-year return in our graph above. However, growth stocks have outperformed their rivals over the last five years.

The high performance with both styles makes eliminating a bit more difficult, so until Aunt Mary can learn more, she will look at funds that invest in all three: growth, value, and blend stocks.

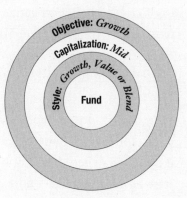

What investment style would you choose? Fill in your target.

Let's Put It All Together Again

So far, Aunt Mary has been able to make some important choices based on what is happening in the market today.

She has chosen a fund with a growth objective and a mid-capitalization. But she is not yet sure whether she is going to go value, growth, or blend in terms of style. How did she make these choices again? Let's recap:

1. *Objective: Growth or income?* To determine objective, you ask yourself the question: Do I want to invest so I can begin to receive income now (which would make you an *income investor*) or am I willing not to touch any of the

money and just let it grow for a period of two years or longer (which would make you a *growth investor*)?

2. *Capitalization: Small-, medium-, or large-cap companies?* To determine which size company has shown the most growth in recent years, you need to take a look at the indexes that represent each one. Check the performance of these indexes on the Internet by going to www.indexfunds.com to help you gauge how the market trend favors each company size. You are looking for the words *small, medium,* or *large*. Make a note of the most popular among the top five choices.

3. *Investment Style: Value, growth, or blend?* Go to www. indexfunds.com and check out what the leading indexes have done over the years. Look for the words *value, growth,* or *blend,* and make a note of the one that appears most often among the top five.

Following these steps, we have been able to do some major eliminating so far. Now that Aunt Mary has narrowed down her pool of possible funds to those with a growth objective; a mid-cap size; and a possible value, growth, or blend investment style, she has managed to bring down the number of possible fund candidates from over 12,000 to barely 1,000 funds!

But we still have the inner ring of the target to fill in. So take out your magnifying glass, because in the next chapter, you and Aunt Mary and I are going to look more closely at a mutual fund report. Then we will be able to identify the numbers that will determine whether or not a fund makes it into our final countdown.

CHAPTER SEVEN

Finding the Needle in the Haystack

Susan stepped out of the Golden Gem jewelry store with confidence. In her hand, she clutched the bag that held her precious cargo. She felt good about her purchase. Diamonds were indeed a girl's best friend, Susan thought, and she felt accomplished and rewarded not only for having had the discipline to save toward this purchase but also for her diligence in her research. She suppressed a giggle as she thought of the look on the salesperson's face when she had commented on the cut, the carats, the clarity, and the color—all factors she knew were essential to consider when buying a diamond. She had studied her four *C*s before venturing out to find *her* perfect diamond, and she had in fact bought a nearly perfect one. Her hard work had paid off.

It also pays to do your homework in your search for the perfect mutual fund for you. But instead of four *C*s, you will need to remember to check out the second part of my system: *The Five Rs: Return, Rank, Ratings, Risk,* and *Ratio.* We will go through The Five *R*s in detail in this chapter. Just sit back, get a cuppa Joe, and read it through. In the next chapter, you will get a chance to put the process into practice.

Having narrowed down your choices of mutual funds among the nine possible categories associated with the size of the company and the investment style of the fund manager, the next step is to look inside the workings of each fund in order to identify those that stand out among their peers by having had the most consistent returns. After all, you are not playing Russian roulette with your financial future. Having to pop Dramamine to endure a mutual fund's up and down swings should not be part of your usual investment experience.

There are several reliable sources where you can find the information you need to evaluate individual mutual funds, but no matter where you go, chances are you will come across one of the most reputable and readily accessible reporting authorities: Morningstar, Inc.

Morningstar has been providing investors with independent information to help in making personal investment decisions since 1984. You may have seen advertising for a certain mutual fund on TV or in magazines in which the fund boasts about its Morningstar rating. Private investors, financial planners, and respected media sources cite the findings of Morningstar as the authority in mutual fund reporting. You can find Morningstar mutual fund reports in most public libraries and on the Internet at www.morningstar.com.

While no single measurement can predict with 100 percent accuracy how volatile or profitable a mutual fund will be in the future, studies have shown that past performance and risk measures *are* good indicators of how each fund will most likely behave in the future. But which ones of the overwhelming number of factors covered in a mutual fund report should you look at to evaluate the merits of a fund? This is where The Five *R*s make their grand entrance.

R Is for *Return*

The first *R* stands for *return*. Return is the profit that the mutual fund has generated in the past. "Wait a minute!" Aunt Mary says. "You said before in chapter 5 that there are three ways I can make money with my mutual funds: dividends, capital gains, and an increase in share price. Which one should I look for?" We want to look at all three, and that's what is referred to as the *total return*.

Total return is regarded as the best measure of fund performance because it is the most comprehensive. It takes into account how much a fund paid out in dividends (if any), how much it paid in capital gains (which are the gains the fund manager made when selling shares owned by the fund), and the growth of the fund's share price.

A mutual fund expresses all these gains as a percentage of an initial investment in a fund and assumes that dividends and capital gains distributions were reinvested in the fund rather than taken out in cash.

"*Argh!* Scary investment language!" Aunt Mary exclaims. "Greek to me!"

Don't worry, keep reading, it will become clearer.

For example: Let's say that you invest $1,000 in a mutual fund. Sometime during that first year, your fund distributes $200 in dividends or capital gains. Instead of cashing in that $200, you *reinvest* the money into your account by buying more shares of the fund. Then, in the meantime, the share value of the stocks in the fund also goes up, so your account increases in value because of that as well. By the year's end, the number of shares you own, times their *new* price per share, is now $1,300. Cool.

Now, how do you then figure out the total return you received on this account over the year? Well, your mutual fund manager will actually do the math for you and report your total return amount. But it's good to know how he or she gets that information. So take out your calculator.

Punch in your ending balance: $1,300

Subtract your initial deposit: $1,000

You get: $300 (this is your profit)

Now divide your profit by your initial deposit: $300 ÷ $1,000 = .30

Multiply times 100 to get a percentage: .30 × 100 = 30%

Your total return is 30 percent

"Wow!" says Aunt Mary. "Sign me up with that one! A 30 percent return sure beats the measly 4 percent I got on my investments last year!"

Not so fast! Before we let Aunt Mary run out of the house, checkbook in hand, to put her hard-earned money into this "stellar" fund, let me tell you that twelve months is a very short period of time in the life of a mutual fund and *definitely* too short a period on which to base a decision of whether or not to invest in it.

Any mutual fund can get lucky in the short term and show tremendous gains. Any mutual fund can also bomb over a short term and lose a lot of money. That's the way it goes.

The true merits of a mutual fund rest on its being able to *consistently, over time*, show the best returns. Those that do are the mutual funds in which we can entrust our investment money. Remember that when looking at total return on our money, it is important to identify which fund *consistently* surpasses the competition. Successful mutual fund investors base their investment decisions on historic average returns, and keep short-term gains or losses in perspective. I cannot stress the importance of this enough.

Successful mutual fund investors base their investment decisions on historic average returns, and keep short-term gains or losses in perspective.

So look closely at a mutual fund report and check out its total return for the last three, five, even ten years. Most financial experts agree that the three-year return is the most significant period to consider because it offers a long enough time span while still showing relevance to the current market conditions.[1] Even so, it is helpful to see how your fund has fared over longer periods of time. If you see that your fund has kept its three-year returns stable during even longer periods of time, it may serve

---

[1] This three-year benchmark provides one of the reasons that I advise you not to invest money you will need access to in less than two years.

as a confirmation of the stability of your fund's returns. If, on the other hand, you find that your fund seems to give erratic returns over different periods of time, it may be a sign that you are looking at a very volatile candidate.

Here is a total return table for a mutual fund as shown in a Morningstar Quicktake® Report.

Trailing Total Return	
	Total Return %
1 Year	54.57
3-Year Annualized	-4.81
5-Year Annualized	-12.51
10-year Annualized	-6.44
Source: www.morningstar.com	

This fund, which has been around for ten years, showed a total return of 54 percent over the past year. But if you took a closer look, you would have seen that the average total return of the fund was an average loss of 4.81 percent per year over the last three years and an average loss of 12.5 percent per year over the past five years! (The word *annualized* in the chart just means averaged.) This is a perfect example of why you cannot rely on a short-term total return to make your mutual fund investment decisions. Remember, you are in it for the long term. Look for a fund that shows a long-term record with positive returns. The average should have smoothed out any temporary negative returns.

R Is for *Ranking*

Remember how happy you felt after buying that perfect sofa in your favorite department store's postholiday sale? Not only was the color right and the size exact, but the price was well within your budget. You congratulated yourself on your prowess as a smart shopper.

Then the inevitable happened. As you sipped your Sunday morning cup of coffee, you casually opened the paper, and there it was! Same style, same size, same color, better manufacturer, and *half the price!* You wanted to die!

Mutual fund investors may be satisfied with a fund's historical total return, but looking at each individual fund's return without further comparison shopping may prove very disappointing.

This is where the use of *benchmarks* comes in handy. No, you don't sit on these guys, but you do use them as measuring sticks against which you measure your mutual fund's performance.

We already touched on the concept of benchmarks when we discussed what indexes do. Benchmarks are measuring sticks against which we can compare a fund to other funds in its peer group. Benchmarks provide perspective. So first you judge a fund on its merits (*R* is for *return*). Then you judge it against its peers (here, *R* is for *ranking*). For example, S&P's Mid-Cap 400 Index is the benchmark for all mid-capitalization stocks in the U.S. stock market. The Standard & Poor's 500 Index, probably the most popular index, represents a benchmark for large-cap companies.

Each mutual fund report shows you what the fund's total return has been in the past and how it ranks compared to the market in general (usually by comparing it to the S&P 500 Index).[2] The report also shows how it ranks compared to other similar funds. By taking into consideration these two comparisons, you will find out if your fund is among the leaders of the entire stock market and within its peer group. After all, wouldn't you want to be able to choose a fund with the best overall return?

Lipper, Inc. and Morningstar, Inc. are the leading providers of peer group benchmarks, and they report these figures in their mutual fund reports in the form of *rankings*.

Look at the following report from Morningstar[3] and see how this

---

[2] It is every stock fund manager's goal to beat the S&P 500 Index. Therefore, it is an important benchmark for the growth mutual fund market, but, as you can see from the chart, not the only relevant one.

[3] Morningstar does not just rely on the category that each fund assigns itself. Instead, it goes into the stocks and bonds that the fund owns and then assigns the corresponding category to that mutual fund.

fund compares to the market and to its peers. You will notice that, when comparing a mutual fund with all the other funds in the same category, it is given a grade expressed in *percent rank*. The highest possible grade is 1 percent, meaning that the fund has a total return that is among the top 1 percent of its peers. A grade of 100 percent means that the fund's returns rate at the bottom of its peers' pile, beaten by the total return of all the other funds in its category.

Trailing Total Returns			
	Total Return %	+/– S&P 500	% Ranking in Cat.
1 Year	20.04	44.14	1
3-Year Annualized	16.54	14.40	2
5-Year Annualized	24.32	10.48	1
10-Year Annualized	20.23	5.81	1

Source: www.morningstar.com

This mutual fund has had a steady total return over the past ten years. The +/–S&P 500 column shows us whether the fund surpassed (as expressed by a positive number) or underperformed (as expressed by a negative number) the return of the S&P 500 Index during the same period. You can see that this fund consistently outperformed the returns of the S&P 500 Index. The last column shows the ranking of the fund when compared to other funds in its category. This mutual fund has been in the top 1 percent or 2 percent of its peers. Not a bad report card.

When you look at a fund's ranking, aim for a lower percentage—no higher than 10 percent.

R Is for *Rating*—Category Rating

Return is definitely important when measuring a mutual fund's performance. After all, isn't making a profit the reason you would invest in a mutual fund to begin with? Yes, but there are other factors, besides the money, that the mutual fund company may produce, that we need to consider before making an intelligent choice. Not all that shines is gold.

One of these factors is the fund's *rating*. More specifically, the fund's *category rating*. Category rating offers the same perspective as benchmark ranking, but it adds one more dimension to the equation: that of risk. In category rating, the mutual fund company is graded as to how much risk it's willing to take to produce its total return. This is a very useful tool for investors. If we looked at only the profits a fund has generated without taking into consideration the risk assumed by the fund manager to make those profits, we are missing half the picture—and that could change our minds about choosing that particular fund.

This easy-to-read method of fund evaluation helps us identify how prudently a fund invests our money. Category rating is a measurement of how well a fund has balanced risk and return relative to its peers.

Let's assume that you gave your uncle Louie your last $500 as an investment. He takes your money and proceeds to bet all of it on Rosie the Gal, the longest shot in that afternoon's local horse derby. At 100-to-1 odds, if you win, you'll walk away with $50,000! That means that you have one chance in one hundred to win. Nice return on your investment, but the chances of winning are pretty dang slim. Uncle Louie would receive a very poor category rating from Morningstar. He would probably rate a 1—the lowest possible rating—when measuring the risk Uncle Louie has taken with your money compared to the possible return on your money.

There are several independent services that rank mutual funds based on how much risk they take to generate their total returns.

Morningstar, Inc.; Value Line, Inc.; Lipper, Inc.; and Standard & Poor's Corporation are some of the leading services for category ratings, each one offering a little twist on the same theme. We will use one of the most widely used ratings: Morningstar's category ratings.

In order to arrive at this rating, Morningstar takes the return of a fund that has been around for at least three years and processes it through a formula that balances risk and return—a complicated formula that would probably make your eyes roll into the back of your head. The result is then compared to that of all the peers in the group and assigned a grade: five is the best rating, and one is the worst.

This is how a Morningstar mutual fund report shows its category rating:

Morningstar Category	Morningstar Rating
Mid-Cap Value	★★★★★

Source: www.morningstar.com

You use the specific Morningstar® *Category Rating*™ to measure a fund's tendency to risk your money when compared to other funds within our chosen group—for example, within mid-cap value funds.

When researching mutual funds, *we will concentrate on those that have a category rating of five*. If you can find an acceptable rate of return that will get you where you want to go, why should you be willing to gamble with your money?

R Is for *Risk*

Can you feel the hair on the back of your neck rise up a bit when I mention that word? I don't want you to fear risk. I want you to understand it.

Risk does not automatically imply "losing your money." If you invest money in the stock market by opening a mutual fund account and can leave the money alone for a few years, you will perceive the ups and downs of the value of your shares as a normal process. Every mutual fund known to humankind has gone up and down, even the best ones. It is just part of life as an investor that your fund is going to have its great years and its share of bloopers. This is the reason why we look at averages when comparing mutual fund returns. *Never take one isolated year's profit or loss as an indicator of a fund's overall performance.*

Studies have shown that the historical price gyrations of a fund can predict its future swings more reliably than any other mutual fund behavior. So to find out if our fund is a mild-mannered bunny rabbit or a thrill-seeking daredevil, we need to take a peek at what it's done in the past.

The best place to find this information is by looking at the fund's *beta*. "Ugh! Is that Greek?" Aunt Mary exclaims in horror. Yep, beta does happen to be the second letter in the Greek alphabet, but in investment lingo, beta measures the volatility or up/down swings of that investment.

Every investment has a beta rating, and mutual funds are no exception. Beta tells us how much more or less a particular fund deviates from the normal movements of the market.

"Yep, I knew it, this *is* Greek," grumbles Aunt Mary, getting ready to run for the woods. Hang in there. This isn't as bad as it sounds.

The S&P 500 Index represents the stock market as a whole in the United States because its 500 stocks form a sample of the many different industries that make up the stock universe. This index goes up and down each day as the ending price of all its members is plotted on a graph.

Beta is expressed in numbers, and the S&P 500 Index is given a beta rating of one.

For those of you who love the math: When we measure the volatility of any mutual fund (or any stock, for that matter), we compare its swings to that of the S&P 500 Index. For example, a mutual fund with a beta rating of 1.20 shows 20 percent more volatility than the Index. So when the S&P 500 Index goes up by one hundred points, the mutual fund tends to go up by 120 points. If the Index drops 100 points, the fund will decline by 120.

For those of you who detest the math: A beta of less than one represents a mutual fund that is mild in its volatility, while a beta of two is telling you that you better fasten your seat belts, because your fund's gyrations are usually double those of the S&P 500. A high beta may be appropriate for aggressive investors, while a low beta may suit those that are risk-adverse.

We can find the beta in Morningstar's mutual fund reports. *The lower the beta number, the more stable the price of the fund, both upward and downward.* There is no highest or lowest grade. Beta is always measured in relation to the swings of a benchmark. A more aggressive investor may welcome a higher beta because when the good times come, they are good indeed. If you are a light sleeper, on the other hand, you may wish to settle for a potentially lower return, since your mutual fund's value retains some equanimity.

It is helpful to compare your fund's beta not only with the beta of the market in general, but also with the beta of your fund's peers, as represented by any one of the indexes that groups them. For example, if you are researching a mid-cap fund, the S&P may give you an idea of how your fund's beta compares to the S&P 500, but you need to know how your fund fares against the medium-sized company index, too. In the mutual fund world, it pays to find out what your neighbors are doing.

Here is an example of a Morningstar Quicktake® Report showing beta comparisons for a mid-cap fund.

Modern Portfolio Theory Statistics		
	Standard Index	**Best Fit Index**
	S&P 500	Standard & Poor's Midcap 400
beta	0.59	0.54

Source: www.morningstar.com

The beta of this mutual fund is .59 when compared to that of the S&P 500 Index. That means that it can be expected to deviate from the swings in that index, up or down, by about half. The fund has a .54 when compared to the index that represents all mid-cap companies. That number shows the mild nature of this fund, since it reacted about half as much as its own representative index. There is no better or worse beta rating, but remember that the higher the beta, the higher possible returns you may have in your fund when things are going well, but the bigger the losses will be during the inevitable lows.

R Is for *Ratio*

The last *R* you need to consider represents the *ratio* or portion of your profit that is going to pay the fees the mutual fund company charges you to invest your money.

You didn't think they would go through all this trouble for nothing, did you? Mutual fund companies are profit-making organizations. They keep some of the money that they generate in the form of fees that they charge you.

You need to know where a mutual fund can legally hide the fees.

There are four places to look, and here is the term used for each one:

1. Front-end load

2. Back-end load (or redemption fee)

3. Expense ratio

4. 12(b)1 fees

A *front-end load* is a markup the fund tacks on to the price of the share when you buy it. You may recall a mention of a fund's NAV from a previous chapter. The NAV is the price of each share of a mutual fund after it counts the value of all its holdings (stocks or bonds it has) at the end of each trading day, takes out expenses, and then divides this value by the number of shares held by the investors of the fund.

Some mutual fund companies add a sales charge or *commission* to the NAV of their shares and that new price is the one new investors pay. This markup that mutual funds are allowed to tack on is regulated by the SEC, and although they are allowed to increase the share value to new buyers by a margin of up to 9 percent, the front-end load of most funds falls in the 4 percent to 5 percent range. How do you know if a mutual fund has a markup? They publish the higher price in their prospectuses, as well as in the daily newspapers under the heading of *POP*, which stands for *public offering price*. Mutual fund reports will specify the front-end load fees under the list of expenses by clearly labeling it as such.

If you are investing in a front-loaded fund, you will pay the higher share price any time you invest *new* money into the fund; but any dividends or capital gains (reinvested into the fund instead of cashed out) will buy additional shares at the NAV. For example, if you opened your account with $1,000, you would have bought shares at the higher price. If you then receive a $200 dividend from the fund and elect to buy additional shares with that money, your purchase would now be at the NAV price. If you wanted to add an additional $500 to the fund, guess what? Your money would go in at the inflated value.

Mutual fund companies pay commissions to stockbrokers with this money. Can you bypass this fee if you go directly to the mutual fund company and don't deal with the middleman for your initial or subsequent purchases? Nope, you will pay the higher fee no matter how you opened your account.

The second fee is the *back-end load*, also known as the deferred, or redemption fee. This is a fee that is tacked on when you *sell* shares of the fund, rather than when you buy them. You would pay the NAV price for the shares you purchased, but the mutual fund may have a 5 percent fee if you sell during the first year, 4 percent during the second, 3 percent the next, and so on until the penalty disappears after the fifth year with the fund. They usually impose a back-end load to discourage investors from cashing in their funds.

Expense ratio is the cost of doing business. This is the percentage that goes to pay for rent, salaries, utilities, supplies, and all the other fees any business is responsible for. Managers of the fund also get paid from this fee. Expense ratio is an ongoing cost of a mutual fund company.

Finally, the *12(b)1 fee* is also a recurring expense that goes to pay for the fund's advertising and marketing efforts. All those glossy brochures are expensive to produce, and you, lucky you, get to pay the printing charges. In reporting expenses, a mutual fund report may include its

12(b)1 fee in the expense ratio percentage. That is the case with Morningstar.com reports. A click on the left-hand side of the screen, however, shows a breakdown of each of these expenses so you know exactly how your money is being spent up front.

This is how a Morningstar Quicktake® Report shows its expenses:

Fund Details	
Sales Charge %	
Front:	None
Deferred:	None
Expense Ratio %	**1.79**

Source: www.morningstar.com

In this chart, a 1.79 percent expense ratio means that this mutual fund will pay 1.79 percent of its assets per year in expenses. This is not only the fund's expense, it is also *your* expense, since these bills will be paid *before* the profits—if there *are* any profits left over—are paid to you. Obviously, the lower the expenses of a fund, the better, since investors will keep more of the profits. Expect to find a higher expense ratio in stock mutual funds—between 1 percent and 1.5 percent—and a lower expense in bond funds—approximately .50 percent.

A Bonus to The Five R s

So now you are familiar with The Five Rs. But before we review them again, I want to tell you about another little investor's helper.

When the stock market is going up, as we saw during the roaring 1990s, chances are that most stock mutual funds also went along for the ride to unprecedented profits. But what happens if the market goes from a bull (meaning an uptrend in the market) to a bear (when the market loses over 20 percent of its value)? Wouldn't you want to know how your fund has fared? There is a useful measuring stick for this, too. It is appropriately called the *Bear Market Decile Rank*.

This number ranks how each mutual fund has weathered the storm during bad times. It is a figure that is calculated over a five-year period and, with one being the best and ten being the worst, it grades the performance of each mutual fund during down times in the stock market.

This is how the Bear Market Decile Rank is shown in a Morningstar Quicktake® Report:

Volatility Measurements

Bear Market Decile Rank   **10**
Source: www.morningstar.com

This chart definitely illustrates a fair-weather friend. You wouldn't expect this mutual fund to hold its value during a bear, or down, market.

Wrapping It All Up

So now you have it. Choosing a mutual fund is achieved through a process of elimination. We use measuring tools like The Five Rs that help us to achieve this elimination. What we ultimately end up with is a mutual fund (or funds) that best suits us.

To review, to evaluate a mutual fund we need to look at:

1. How the fund has performed in the past. We look at its total *return* over an extended period of time. Choose a fund with consistent positive returns over one that may have a high one-year return and negative average returns over a three- or five-year period.

Trailing Total Returns	
	Total Return %
1 Year	54.57
3-Year Annualized	-4.81
5-Year Annualized	-12.51
10-year Annualized	-6.44

Source: www.morningstar.com

2. How the total return of the fund compares to the return of its peers. We look at its *ranking*. We want to look for funds with a ranking of 10 percent or lower.

Trailing Total Returns			
	Total Return %	**+/– S&P 500**	**% Ranking in Cat.**
1 Year	20.04	44.14	1
3-Year Annualized	16.54	14.40	2
5-Year Annualized	24.32	10.48	1
10-Year Annualized	20.23	5.81	1

Source: www.morningstar.com

3. How the fund finds a balance between the need to generate profits and the risk of losing money. We look at how it's measured by the Morningstar® Rating™. We won't settle for a rating of less than five.

Morningstar Category	Morningstar Rating
Mid-Cap Value	★★★★★

Source: www.morningstar.com

4. How the volatility of the price swings in the past three years stacks up when compared to the market and to its peers, as measured by the fund's beta. We look at a fund's *risk*. The lower the beta, the better.

Modern Portfolio Theory Statistics

	Standard Index	Best Fit Index
	S&P 500	Standard & Poor's Midcap 400
beta	0.59	0.5

Source: www.morningstar.com

5. How the fund imposes fees on our money before we get to it. We look at its *ratio* of the fees it charges against its returns. Look for fees less than 1.44 percent (that's the average as of 6/18/01) in domestic stock funds, and less than 1.85 percent (the average as of 6/18/01) in international stock funds.

Fund Details

Sales Charge %	
Front:	None
Deferred:	None
Expense Ratio %	**1.79**

Source: www.morningstar.com

Bonus: How the fund weathered the stormy bad times in a bear market. We look at the *Bear Market Decile Rank.* The best funds will have a ranking of one or two.

Volatility Measurements

Bear Market Decile Rank	**10**

Source: www.morningstar.com

You've Come a Long Way, Baby

You and Aunt Mary have now learned the entire system that you need to find the one best mutual fund for you from among the 12,300 out there. Using the target and The Five Rs plus the bonus helper will get you to your winning fund. Now all that's left is to practice the system, which we will do together in the next chapter. I will walk you through the process using the Internet.

"Hey, don't call me some batty old lady stuck in her ways, but I simply prefer hard copies to computers," grouses Aunt Mary. "I'm off to the library. See ya on the *QE2*!" Seeing that on-line practice is not her style, we are going to bid Aunt Mary good-bye.

But those of you who like the convenience and speed of the Internet, sit down, turn on your computer, and get ready to find the fund that will fuel your dream.

CHAPTER EIGHT

And the Winner Is . . .

Once upon a time, a severe drought hit the land. All the lakes and streams dried up. Two frogs, searching for water, at last came upon a well. But they could not agree as to whether they should leap in or not. The first frog said, "Yum! Water would sure hit the spot. I think we should just jump in immediately." The second frog demurred. "I'm thirsty, too, but what if this well is dry? Then where will we be?" The first frog pooh-poohed the second one, jumped up on the edge of the well, waved *sayonara*, and jumped in without a glance. He landed with a thump at the bottom of the dried-up well. No water. No way out. The second frog was glad he had not made the leap before looking.

As we saw with the first wave of IPO mania in the late 1990s, jumping right in can have its benefits. But as we also learned in the second wave, doing our research often makes the difference between adding to our financial well or getting all dried up. Lucky for you, you don't have to end up a desiccated frog; you have your golden list of the most important factors to consider when choosing a mutual fund.

In this chapter, we will go through the actual process of choosing a fund together, so that you can see how everything you have learned so far fits together to help you find a winning fund.

At this point, may I suggest that if you haven't already done so, you dedicate a notebook to your investment pursuits? That way, all the research you do in this chapter and the notes you take will be preserved in one place for easy, reliable reference.

Then, to illustrate the steps we are about to go through, since Aunt Mary skipped out on us, we are going to help a fictional couple, Tony and Amanda, find a mutual fund to meet their financial goals. Get out your notebook and let's begin.

Tony and Amanda

Tony and Amanda are thirty-something and have two-year-old twin daughters named Olivia and Chloe. Tony and Amanda had, like other couples they knew, waited until they had great jobs and a home before starting a family. The twins were a welcome—and expensive—surprise. Amanda, being a practical person, thinks they should start doing something about the twins' college fund. Tony says, "Ahh, that's so far off. I am sure if we just remember to put a couple of bucks in a bank account every month, by the time Chloe and Olivia are seventeen and ready to fly the coop, we'll have it covered."

Amanda, trying not to scoff, asks Tony, "Do you know that just tuition at a top-notch college these days can run $25,000 a year—and that's just for one child? Multiply that by two and then again by four for each year of college. Then factor in inflation. By the time the girls are ready for college, we're going to need about $312,000."[1]

Tony's mouth drops open.

Amanda continues. "Even if we got 5 percent on our money, which is the rate of a savings account at Gonif Bank down the street, we would

[1] Amanda used the Inflation Table in chapter 3 (page 39) to determine how inflation would affect how much they needed in their college fund: $25,000 per year, per child, for four years equals $200,000. Amanda estimated a 3 percent inflation rate. After fifteen years, at 3 percent inflation, they would need $200,000 × 1.558 = $311,600, which Amanda rounded up to $312,000.

have to set aside \$1,167[2] a month for the next fifteen years to reach that goal." Tony tries not to choke on his pretzel. "But I know a better way," she says, whipping out her handy investment notebook. "You see, I've been reading this book. . . ."

Make Like Amanda

Take out your notebook and draw your target in the middle of the page like this, or print it out from www.JulieStav.com:

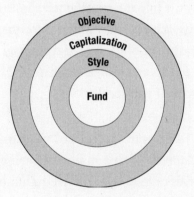

Let's go through each ring in this target with Amanda and Tony to make sure they cover all their bases.[3]

---

[2] Using the Monthly Investment Table in chapter 2 (page 23), Amanda figured out that at 5 percent interest, they would have to save \$3.74 per month to accumulate \$1,000. Since their goal is \$312,000, she divided \$312,000 by 1,000: \$312,000 ÷ 1,000 = 312. She then multiplied that number by \$3.74: 312 × \$3.74 = \$1,166.88, which she rounded off to \$1,167.

[3] As we practice the process of filling in the target in this chapter, we will be using information that is current at the time of this book's printing. When you go to actually use this process, you may find different information and may make different choices. But what you learn in this chapter about *how* to make your choices will still be valid.

Gimme an *O* for *Objective*

"OK, honey," Amanda says, "we know that our goal is to have $312,000 in fifteen years and that there's no way we are getting there with a savings account. This makes us a special type of investor: a growth investor."

Amanda explains to Tony that since their financial goal is fifteen years in the future, they are, first and foremost, long-term investors where Olivia and Chloe's college fund is concerned. If your goal is long term, like Tony and Amanda's, you are in the right place in this book. In Tony and Amanda's case, the length of their goal and the fact that they do not need the money now but at a specific time in the future makes them investors with a *growth objective*; they are in it for the long run.

What is your investment objective? *It depends on how long till you need to start spending your investment money.* In chapter 2, you determined the time frame of your goal. If you recall:

1. If you wish to reach your goal in two years or less, you are a *short-term investor*. Examples of this might be saving for a vacation or a new car in two years or less. You will need a lump-sum distribution of all the money at that time. You don't have a growth investment objective here because:

   a. You are going to need it so soon that investing it makes no sense because you cannot afford to weather the ups and downs of the stock market.

   b. You are cashing it all out at once, and the fund does not need to keep growing so that you can receive monthly income from the interest.

   c. You are talking about an amount of money that is not large enough to make much money in two years unless you take wild risks, an investment approach we do not advocate.

If your goal is two years or less, you have four main savings options that you learned about in chapter 4.

If you wish to reach your goal in two to five years, or once you are two to five years away from what was a long-term goal, you are still considered a short-term investor. However, your objective is a mixed growth *and* income objective. (You still want your money to grow, but since you will be accessing it soon, you want to put some money in more stable, less risky funds that generate some income.) Examples of this type of goal are if you have two to five years to pay off credit card debt, if you are five years or less away from your retirement nest egg goal, or if you are saving for a down payment on a home in five years or less. You will also have a mixed growth and income objective if you have just won the lottery, gotten a severance, or received an inheritance and want to live off the interest. Keep reading, but pay special attention to chapters 10 and 11, which tell you how to invest for income and transition your investment strategy as you count down to your goal.

2. If you wish to achieve your goal in a period of five to ten years, you are a *medium-term investor* with a growth objective. Examples of this could be saving toward a college fund (which could also be a long-term goal if it's more than ten years away) or if you are five or more years away from your retirement goal. In both cases, your objective is growth, because your main purpose in the investment process is to fatten the kitty, not to generate income.

3. *Long-term investors* have a goal that they wish to accomplish in ten or more years. You fall into this category of investor if you are working on your nest egg retirement account and are more than ten years away from it. Again, your objective is growth. Another example might be that you just hit the lottery, got a big inheritance from Great Uncle Jonathan, or got a nice severance check and want to quit work and live off your booty's interest *ten years from now*. You are still a long-term growth investor, and this chapter's for you.

4. Another possibility is that you don't care how long it takes to reach your goal, you don't want to read anymore or learn anything else, you are sick of this whole thing, and you just want to jump on the mutual fund bandwagon. If this sounds like you, read the section in chapter 5 on index funds and ETFs, and good-bye.

You might have goals in all of these categories, in which case, the bad news is that you're gonna have to read the rest of this book. The good news is that when you do, you will know what it will take to reach all of those goals!

Back to our thirty-something couple, where Tony has finally caught his breath. Because Tony and Amanda's objective is growth, they have already eliminated all bond funds. How's that?

Bond funds (also called *fixed-income funds*) are short-distance runners. Amanda and Tony might consider them as they get closer to their end goal, but for now, they want the most powerful performer: one that can go the distance. And when it comes to long-distance running, you just can't beat mutual funds that invest in stocks. So they will concentrate their search on stock-based mutual funds. Amanda and Tony fill in the Objective ring with the word *growth*.

What is *your* objective? Is it growth or income? Fill in the Objective ring with your answer.

Gimme a *C* for *Capitalization*

To fill out the next ring in the target, we need to do some research. If you are not on-line, you may find the information in reports provided by Value Line, Inc.; Lipper, Inc.; or Morningstar, Inc. at your local library. I will walk you through the steps using the Internet.

This step requires choosing among large-, mid-, and small-cap companies.

In order to see how each one of these groups has fared in the past, go to www.indexfunds.com. In the "Data Central" subheading, open the drop-down box and click on "Indexes." At the top of this page, you will see a drop-down box with the heading "Sort by;" within this drop-down window, we will choose "3-Year Returns" since this time period is considered by most experts to represent a reasonable sampling of recent history in a fund's performance.

Click on the boxes next to "Large Cap," "Mid Cap," and "Small Cap," so that there are checks in each of the three boxes. These are the three categories you would like to rank. Ignore all the rest of the boxes and windows. Then click on the "Screen!" button at the very bottom of the page.

Here is what Tony and Amanda found when they did this. (**Remember, your results may be different.**)

Index Name	Category	3 Yr	1 Mo	3 Mo	YTD	1 Yr	5 Yr	10 Yr
Dow Jones Mid Cap Value	Value	29.99	1.19	8.77	−0.20	9.40	16.88	17.35
Barra Mid Cap Value	Value	27.84	−3.31	11.32	1.00	11.04	17.05	~
Wilshire Mid Cap Value	Value	24.91	−0.82	10.11	0.12	8.18	15.26	18.11
Dow Jones Small Value	Value	24.28	1.23	14.92	1.46	4.10	13.86	16.70
Wilshire Small Cap Value	Value	23.21	−0.01	13.55	2.34	4.15	12.88	18.05
Russell 2000 Value	Value	22.81	−0.14	13.65	2.62	4.22	12.59	17.64

Source: www.indexfunds.com

Take a look at the Index Name column. Move your finger down, and write down the first five names on your list. Tony and Amanda wrote down: Dow Jones Mid Cap Value, Barra Mid Cap Value, Wilshire Mid Cap Value, Dow Jones Small Value, and Wilshire Small Cap Value.

Looking at this list of top performing indexes, Amanda notices that the word *mid* keeps repeating itself. That means that mid-cap stocks were among the top five leaders when compared with their cousins, the large- and the small-caps, during the past three years. Tony and Amanda are going to concentrate their search on mid-cap companies and fill in the word *mid-cap* in the Capitalization ring of the target. Take note of what appears on your list. Are there mostly mid-caps? Small-caps? Whatever shows up most, that is what you're going to concentrate your search on, *because that is what the market suggests*. On to the next ring in the target.

Gimme an *S* for *Style*

The next ring on the target is Style. Amanda knows that means they have to find out which investment style was most productive during the past three years. A *growth investment style* fund concentrates on stocks with great earnings potentials. The stock price of these companies is usually higher because they are popular with other investors as well, but the mutual funds with a growth investment style do not mind paying more for them because they believe these companies will continue to have stellar earnings. And stellar earnings in stocks usually translate to share price increases.

A *value investment style* fund focuses on bargains, investing in stocks that are out of favor but have tremendous potential in the long run. Mutual fund companies that follow this investment philosophy go out of their way to find fallen stars, buy their shares cheap, and hold onto them in the hopes that their price will go up.

A *blend investment style* combines characteristics of both growth and value. This mutual fund company invests in both companies that have good earnings and pricey shares as well as out-of-favor wanna-bes that the fund believes will resurrect in time.

It's back to the computer screen. This time, Amanda counts how many times she sees the words *value, growth,* or *blend* in the top five performers under the Category column. Which one dominates? Value seems to be the leader in this particular example—a clear sign that the public (and other mutual funds) have been bargain hunting. Since the word *value* is seen repeatedly, it gives her an indication that value-oriented stocks showed the highest returns during the past three years. It follows that mutual funds that concentrate on this winning group also reaped the benefits. So, in the investment Style ring of the target, Tony and Amanda fill in the word *value*.

So far, Tony and Amanda have narrowed their search to stock funds in mid-cap companies with a value investment style. What are *your* criteria so far? What did you see on your screen, and therefore what did you put in the Style ring of your target?

Gimme an *F* for *Fund*

Even though we've narrowed the field quite a bit, it's now time to get down to specifics. It is time to proceed to the bull's-eye in your target.

In order to identify which mutual fund is the one that has the best potential to get us where we want to go with the least amount of risk, we will have to do some research. The easiest way is to use the Morningstar, Inc. web site to guide us through our search, but if you don't have access to a computer, you can find the information in reports provided by Value Line, Inc.; Lipper, Inc.; or Morningstar, Inc. at your local library.

Follow along with Tony and Amanda as they go to www.morningstar. com to continue their research. Now scroll down the middle of the screen to "Mutual Fund Screener." This screen is a *filtering screen*, meaning that it will show you a list of mutual funds that meet specific criteria.

An uninformed investor might not have a clue as to what to look for, but not Tony and Amanda—and not you, either! Tony and Amanda have done their homework, and they came to this screen well prepared, already knowing what they wanted: *the best mid-cap value mutual fund*. By now you, too, know what you want and have narrowed down your choice. So let's tackle this next step together, using Amanda and Tony's example.

This is what Morningstar's Mutual Fund Screener screen looks like:

Set Criteria		
Fund Type Fund group:	All	
Morningstar Category:	All	
Manager tenure greater than or equal to:	Any	

Source: www.morningstar.com

The first section of the screen asks for the Fund Type. The choices are: Fund group, Morningstar Category, and Manager tenure.

We are not looking for any particular fund group family—everybody gets a chance to compete—so leave that drop-down window with the "All" in it alone.

Click on the Morningstar Category drop-down menu. Since Tony and Amanda are looking for a mid-cap value fund, they clicked on "Mid Value." ("Mid Value" represents the mid-cap value mutual funds.) Tony and Amanda have just told Morningstar, Inc. that they wish to see all mid-cap value mutual funds. **Choose the type of fund you are looking for.**

Skip the "Manager tenure greater than or equal to:" drop-down window. We don't know anything about any particular managers. We'll let all of them compete for our money. So leave the "Any" alone in this drop-down window.

Scroll down. We will get to the details of the funds as we look deeper into each one, but for now, we want to sort any candidate by fund objective, investment style, and risk. So skip the "Cost and Purchase" section. Keep going till you get to the "Ratings and Risk" section of the Morningstar screen. It should look something like this:

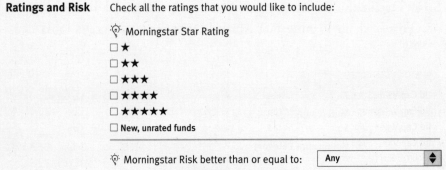

Source: www.morningstar.com

On this screen, we get to choose the Morningstar® Star Category Rating™ of the mutual fund of our choice. If you recall, this rating will show us how the mutual funds, graded on a bell curve, rate among their peers in balancing their return and their risk.

In the Morningstar® Star Rating™, the highest possible rating is five stars, and the least is one star. We want to see the top of the class, so let's ask for a Star Rating of five. Check the box next to the five stars.

Scroll down in this section till you reach "Morningstar Risk better than or equal to." This measures the downside volatility of the mutual fund when compared to its peers. Huh? In English, that just means that it measures how your fund compares to other funds like it when it comes to riding the ups and downs in price along the way. Open the drop-down menu, and click on the words "Below Average." You do *not* want to start your search with a fund candidate that's gonna require megadoses of Valium. Stability is a highly regarded quality among the best-performing mutual funds. You are better off with a mutual fund that shows a stable path than one that has tremendous highs in price but then sinks down into oblivion. This is not Russian roulette.

Now skip the "Returns" and "Portfolio" sections, which we will cover in detail as we narrow our list to the real potential candidates. Go to the very bottom of the screen. Click on the "Show Results" button. *Voilà!* What you now see is a choice of mutual funds that meets your chosen criteria. This is what Amanda and Tony's list looked like:

▼ Fund Name	Morningstar Category	Morningstar Rating	YTD Return (%)	Expense Ratio (%)	Net Assets ($ mil)
Mid Cap Value Fund A	Mid Value	★★★★★	0.37	1.25	4
Mid Cap Value Fund B	Mid Value	★★★★★	-0.53	1.26	0
Mid Cap Value Fund C	Mid Value	★★★★★	-0.45	1.26	1
Mid Cap Value Fund D	Mid Value	★★★★★	-0.16	1.24	2,394

Source: Fictitious chart based on information found in www.morningstar.com. For illustrative purposes only.

As you can see, the fund names on this list are made up. I have created fictitious names in order to abide with SEC regulations, which prevent me from recommending any mutual fund without giving you a prospectus and establishing personal suitability for you. All the regulatory bodies that look over my shoulder would frown heavily at the thought I that might be recommending a specific mutual fund to you without first going through the necessary steps of assessing your personal financial circumstances. So we balance their legitimate concern with our legitimate need to go the final step and learn to compare among funds, by going through the comparison process with a real set of funds that have been assigned fake names. Your chart on the Morningstar web site will offer the same information categories, but it will contain actual mutual fund names.

Going back to Tony and Amanda's list, we can see that there are four mutual funds here that meet their criteria.

For now, I want to ignore the numbers in the last three columns. We will first look into each specific mutual fund report to identify the main characteristics of each fund.

In order to keep track of our findings, we will make a mutual fund scorecard with the factors that ought to be considered. This scorecard will help us compare the funds and make a final decision by collecting all the pertinent information in one place. Since we are going to be using quite a few of these scorecards, you can print out blank ones from www.JulieStav.com, photocopy them, create them on your computer, or simply draw them up in your investment notebook.

Under Fund Name, Amanda and Tony write down the name of the first fund to be considered: Fund A. On your scorecard, you enter the name of your first fund. Then, back at the computer, click on the first mutual fund on your list. You will be taken to the detailed Morningstar Quicktake® Report for that fund.

FUND CANDIDATES SCORECARD

Fund Name	Total Return						Beta		Fees				Bear Market Decile Rank
	1-Yr Return	Net 1-Yr Return*	3-Yr Return	5-Yr Return	3-Yr % Rank	Cat. Rating	Vs. S&P 500	Vs. Best Fit Index	Front-end	Back-end	Expense Ratio	12 (b)1	

*The Net 1-Year Return represents the one-year return minus any front-end or back-end fees. Morningstar's 1-Year Return figures already reflect the Expense Ratio and 12(b)1 fee, so we don't need to subtract them again.

Remember The Five R s?

Now let's go over the list of Rs. The first *R* is for *Total Returns*. Look at the left navigational bar of your mutual fund report and find the heading labeled "Total Returns." Click on it.

Scroll down to "Trailing Total Returns." In the Trailing Returns section, you will have the most updated information available for this fund. The word *trailing* means that as they add new information, the old information is dropped. For example, the one-year total return includes the return for the previous twelve months, updated each month. Here's what showed up on Tony and Amanda's computer.

Trailing Total Returns

	Total Return %	+/– S&P 500	% Rank in Cat.
➤ 1-Year	28.68	47.07	12
➤ 3-Year Annualized	17.34	13.85	3
➤ 5-Year Annualized	---	---	---
➤ 10-Year Annualized	---	---	---

Data through 04-13-01
10-Year through 03-31-01

Source: www.morningstar.com

We will concentrate on the one-year, three-year annualized, and five-year annualized returns to get a clear perspective of the stability of this mutual fund. Remember: Most smart investors give more weight to the three-year return figures.

Find the one-year, three-year, and five-year total returns for your first fund, and write them in your scorecard under the proper headings. (For now, skip the "Net 1-Yr Return" column. We will go back to it momentarily.) Notice that this fund does not have a five-year return. That's because it has not been in existence that long. If this is the case with the fund on your screen, mark a dash in the five-year return box.

Our next *R* is for Total Return *Percent Rank*. You will find this number on the far right column of the Trailing Total Returns report.

Fund A had a 12 percent rating in the ranking for the past year and a 3 percent for the past three years. That means that this fund's return rated in the upper 12 percent of all mid-cap value funds during the past twelve months and had an average ranking of 3 percent for the past three years. Tony and Amanda will record the three-year figure of 3 percent in the "3-yr % Rank" column of their scorecard. Write the three-year percent rank on your scorecard. We are done with the Trailing Total Returns table.

Go back to the first page of this fund's Morningstar Quicktake® Report by clicking once on the Back button of your browser. The next box on our scorecard asks for the fund's Morningstar® Rating™, the third R on our list. Find that section on your report. It should look like this:

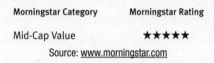

Morningstar Category	Morningstar Rating
Mid-Cap Value	★★★★★

Source: www.morningstar.com

If you recall, when we filled in the original screen from Morningstar, we requested all funds with a category rating of five stars, so this should be the number you find in all the reports that you research.

Tony and Amanda write down on their scorecard the category rating for this fund. That grade is a five. Write down your fund's category rating.

The fourth R is Risk. Look in the navigational sidebar of your Morningstar report. Click on "Risk Measures." That screen will show you what you need to know to evaluate your fund's personality. Is your fund an even-tempered one or one that will have mood (and price) swings that may keep you up at night? This is where beta comes in handy. Check it out.

Modern Portfolio Theory Statistics

	Standard Index S&P 500	Best Fit Index Standard & Poor's MidCap 400
beta	0.52	0.47

Source: www.morningstar.com

Tony and Amanda's mutual fund had a rating of .52 when compared to the swings of the S&P 500 Index, and a .47 when compared to the index that best resembles the stocks within it (the S&P MidCap 400 Index). That means that the volatility of the fund over the past thirty-six months has been just a hair over half (as indicated by the .52 grade) that of the general market, and a little less than half (as indicated by the .47) the volatility of the 400 stocks that form the S&P MidCap 400 Index. This rates this fund as a mild-mannered candidate. Tony and Amanda write in these two numbers in the appropriate places on their scorecard. You also should write the two beta ratings on your fund's report in the appropriate boxes of your scorecard.

Now let's look at the last *R: Ratio*, otherwise known as the portion of your profit that goes toward paying the fees the mutual fund company *charges you* to invest your money. In other words, what part of the money generated do you get to keep for yourself? For that, we look at the four places where any fund can hide expenses that will dilute your profits. After all, if there is a cover charge to get in, the party better be worth it.

Again in the Morningstar.com navigational sidebar to the left, you will find "Fees and Expenses." Click there. This is the table that popped up for Tony and Amanda:

Fees and Expenses

Maximum Sales Fees		Total Cost Projections (per $10,000)	
Initial	None	3-Year	$1101
Deferred	None	5-Year	$2128
Redemption	None		

Source: www.morningstar.com

Notice that this fund does not have a *front-end* fee (labeled *initial* fee here) and no *back-end* fees (aka *deferred* or *redemption fees*). Tony and Amanda can write zeros in the columns under fees that correspond to these charges on their scorecard. Does your fund have front-end or back-end fees?

If there are any front- or back-end fees, add them up and subtract that number from the total one-year return number you had written down. *The total return figures in Morningstar Quicktake® Reports do not reflect these charges, and because you want to know how much you really get to keep, you must adjust the total return in order to account for the load that you paid.* Go back to the "Net 1-Yr Return" column and write down this net amount.

We are missing two additional possible fees: *expense ratio* and *12(b)1 fees.* They are also listed under fees and expenses. Look at the actual fees of the fund, rather than the maximum fees they *could* charge; we want specifics. Here's what Tony and Amanda found:

Fees and Expenses

Maximum Fees		Actual Fees	
Administrative	0.00%	12b-1	0.00%
Management	0.70%	Management	0.70%
12(b)1	0.00%	Total Expense Ratio	1.25%

Source: www.morningstar.com

As you can see, there is no 12(b)1 fee. Also, the total expense ratio is 1.25 percent. The expense ratio in a Morningstar report is taken from the fund's annual report and reflects *all* the fees imposed on the fund. This is the grand total, including 12(b)1 fees, management and administrative charges, and anything else the fund spent money on. So make sure not to count the 12(b)1 or other fees twice, since they are already included when you see a number for total expense ratio.

Fill in the 12(b)1 fee and total expense ratio of your fund on your scorecard. *But since these expenses are already accounted for before the total return numbers are reported by Morningstar, we do not need to adjust our total return results any further.*

It is important to look at a fund's fees because you only get to keep the difference between the total return percentage and the fees the fund takes out of these returns before passing them on to you. In the case of Mid Value Fund A, the mutual fund had an annual average total return of 17.34 percent during the past three years, and its expense ratio was 1.25 percent. That means that the fund really returned 18.59 percent (17.34 percent plus 1.25 percent). Investors only saw the 17.34 percent reflected in their profits as a result of this fund's maintenance cost. It is important for you as an investor to make sure that the investments in your mutual funds are paying off *and* that these profits are not being siphoned off by the overhead of the fund. How a mutual fund company controls its fees is a good indication of the general health and stability of the fund. Always find out what the fees are, and compare them as you consider your mutual fund options.

We are almost done. Let's find out the bonus question for our fund: How has it fared during a bear (down) market? This number, called the *Bear Market Decile Rank*, is calculated over a five-year period. Click on the "Risk Measures" heading on the navigational bar; it will lead you to the same page where you found the beta rating of the fund.

This is what Tony and Amanda found regarding the Bear Market Decile Rank of Mid Cap Value Fund A:

Bear Market Decile Rank*   ---
*Trailing 5-year through 03-31-01
Source: www.morningstar.com

Since there is no number for this entry, we know that this fund did not have five-year total return figures. It has not been in existence that long. What is the Bear Market Decile Rank of your fund? Write it in your scorecard.

There it is! YOU DID IT! You just accomplished the hardest part of

investing in mutual funds: You have identified and used the most important factors to consider when evaluating a mutual fund.

There is plenty of additional information in a mutual fund report.
Take some time to peruse the description of the fund, its top holdings
(what the mutual fund owns), the minimum amount required to open
an account, how long the manager has been at the helm (after all, you
don't want to find out that the person who was responsible for generating these great results has just retired and there is a new whipper-
snapper in her place, taking the credit for the old manager's efforts),
etc. The more familiar you become with these reports, the better off
you'll be.

Now it's time to fill out the scorecard on your own. Fill out your
scorecard with all the information on the top four funds you found as a
result of your initial screening. Fill out the row of numbers on each
fund just as you did with this first practice fund. When you're done,
we'll go through the rest of the process with Amanda and Tony's fund
choices to show you how to compare your top choices and reach a final
decision.

Here is what Amanda and Tony's scorecard looks like:

FUND CANDIDATES SCORECARD

Fund Name	Total Return					Cat. Rating	beta		Fees				Bear Market Decile Rank
	1-Yr Return	Net 1-Yr Return*	3-Yr Return	5-Yr Return	3-Yr % Rank		Vs. S&P 500	Vs. Best Fit Index	Front-end	Back-end	Expense Ratio	12 (b)1	
A	28.68	28.68	17.34	-	3	5	.52	.47	0	0	1.25	0	-
B	20.00	20.00	21.65	-	1	5	.56	.56	0	0	1.24	0	1
C	22.26	16.51	23.43	4.50	1	5	.96	.96	5.75	0	1.36	.35	5
D	21.16	21.16	19.05	23.73	1	5	.53	.53	0	0	1.19	0	1

*The Net 1-Year Return represents the one-year return minus any front-end or back-end fees. Morningstar's 1-Year Return figures already reflect the Expense Ratio and 12(b)1 fee, so we don't need to subtract them again.

At this point in the process, when we are beginning our final analysis, we need to get the prospectuses on each fund we are looking at. For that, we either call the fund and request one or go to www.sec.gov/edgar/ searchedgar/prospectus.htm and type in the name of each fund. Make sure to print out the prospectus for each fund and read it. (As you review your prospectuses, remember that the information on your scorecard reflects your fund's last day's closing prices, while your fund's prospectus may reflect an older cutoff date. This may explain any discrepancy you find between the results reported by these two information sources.)

A prospectus includes information on how to open an account, how to purchase or redeem shares, and how to contact shareholder services for each specific fund. You will also find the fund objective and the type of stock or bonds in which it invests. And in the risk section of the prospectus, you will be able to read whether the fund is considered to be risky or conservative. Fees, past performance of the fund, and how management is planning to generate future profits are also found in this document. While important information resides in a prospectus, if you are having trouble falling asleep, you will probably do well by reading one. I bet you'll be out like a light in no time. I recommend learning the system in this book and using the prospectus to fill in where needed.

Know also that the information you have written down on your scorecard is not meant to replace a prospectus. The scorecard is only an instrument to help you narrow down your investment choices. You should use *both* tools to gain as much information as possible about the fund in which you are about to invest your precious, hard-earned money.

The Final Countdown

Tony and Amanda did all that work and have filled out their scorecard. They downloaded and read the prospectus for each fund. What now?

The easiest way to go about picking the right fund is using the process of elimination. First you want to eliminate the fund you like the *least*.

Look at the consistency of returns of all the funds in your scorecard. Is the three-year annualized total return consistent with that of its one-year and five-year annualized? If the fund has not been around for five years, does that bother you? It's not necessarily a bad sign, but it does mean that you can't have access to the numbers that reflect how the fund performed over a longer period of time. This is particularly important when you consider factors like the Bear Market Decile Rank, which is calculable only over a five-year period. With all things being equal, choose a fund with more longevity. Look at the beta. How much risk are you willing to take? And check out the fees against the total return. Higher fees could mean less money in your pocket.

Notice that Fund C on Tony and Amanda's scorecard has a good track record for the last three years but seemed to fall apart in the five-year column. What happened? Look at its Bear Market Decile Rank. Its grade is a fairly low grade for that category: a 5 percent. Its beta, indicating risk, is the highest of all the listed funds, with a rating of .96. It also has the highest fees, which will eat up your profits before you ever see them. This would be my last choice from this list.

On the other hand, look at the merits of Fund D. Its beta is one of the lowest, and its returns have been steady over the past five years. It rates a 1 percent during a bear market, the best ranking. Its fees are the lowest, with a 1.19 percent expense ratio. I would rate this fund at the top of my list.

Fund B has no five-year returns, but it fared well in one- and three-total returns. It has a low beta and the second lowest fees. This would be my second choice.

Fund A has a good one-year return, but we don't consider that a good indicator of future performance. So we look at its return and ranking for the three-year total returns, which are lower. Its beta is the lowest of the bunch, but so are its three-year returns. This comes in as third runner-up on Tony and Amanda's scorecard.

Rank the funds on your scorecard. What if two funds seem too close to call? Maybe you have a tie between two of them. Read on.

Tiebreakers

Sometimes two funds will seem equally appealing. That's where tiebreakers come in. A tiebreaker between two good funds might be something as simple as an automatic disqualification because the minimum amount required by one of them is not within your budget. For example, when Tony and Amanda read the prospectus for what they believe is their third choice, Mid Value Fund A, they find that it requires an initial deposit of one million dollars. That fact alone can definitely disqualify this fund for many of us; it certainly does for Tony and Amanda. That is why it is so important to read the prospectus of a fund before you make your final decision.

If you want to check out the qualifications of a particular fund, you can look up an isolated mutual fund report by typing the fund's nickname—or ticker symbol—in the box at the top of the Morningstar home page.

So go back and type in the ticker symbol for each fund you have on your list. If you don't know the symbol, type in the first few letters of the name of your fund, and you will be given a list of funds from which to choose, along with the symbol for each fund.

When the funds pop up on the screen, go to each fund's Morningstar Quicktake® Report. Click on the "Purchase Info" link in the navigational sidebar on the left-hand side of your computer screen. Is the fund's initial purchase one that you would or could consider? If it isn't, disqualify that mutual fund. Notice that most funds require a lower initial amount for IRAs (Individual Retirement Accounts) because you don't take the money out of IRAs for a while, so the fund managers know they can count on having your money for a while. Also, most funds either lower or eliminate their initial requirement if you are willing to go on an automatic investment plan where your deposit is transferred from your bank account to the fund each month. You will find this information in the prospectus.

How else can you break a tie? Look at the funds' top holdings. You might find that between the two funds there is a very close resemblance in the stocks they own. To choose one over the other, you go into the details. You may also find that a particular fund owns shares of a company in which you do not, for personal or other reasons, want to invest. This could be the case if, for instance, you want to invest only in companies that are socially responsible. Try comparing their betas; the volatility factor may also make a fund lose out.

Regardless of your personal interests, you can always make a decision based on the details you find out about two funds. As the saying goes: Greatness is in the details.

Almost There

With your ranked scorecard in hand, I strongly urge you to go on-line and read about your company in detail, or like Aunt Mary, do so at the library. *Read those prospectuses!* You can also find articles written about your fund on Morningstar.com. Take the time to click on as much information as you can about each of your candidates. And take notes. The more you know about all the funds you look at, the better off you'll be.

Ultimately, choosing a mutual fund is like choosing a mate. You may have a list of requirements based on solid physical and spiritual criteria, but even when you think you have met the perfect person who meets every requirement on your checklist—the one and only one for you—it all eventually boils down to a subjective decision on your part.

If you are worrying about entering into matrimony with a fund that does not turn out to be the lifetime partner you thought it would, do not despair. Even though you have made an educated choice and a mutual fund represents a medium- to long-term investment, there may be reasons why you would choose to sell your fund and move on to another. One of these reasons might be that you need to adjust your investing style because you are getting closer to your goals and do not need to be as financially aggressive. Another reason may be that your investment goals have changed (for instance, perhaps in ten years, Amanda and Tony discover that they actually need to have more money than they anticipated to cover the rest of the college expenses for their twins, or perhaps they live in a state that has a great state college system, and they find that they need less). Whatever the case, it behooves you to check up on your investments every once in a while.

To keep you in sync with your investment choices, you will periodically check up on your mutual funds. You don't need to worry about every cough and hiccup of the market, so you need not check up on them daily, weekly, or even monthly as you need to with individual stocks. But do make sure to update your financial goals at least once a year so that you make sure the funds you chose still meet your needs. By occasionally reminding yourself of the reason you invested in your fund (or funds) to begin with, you will make sure the romance in your mutual fund investment relationship is kept alive. The next chapter tells you how to go about your periodic checkup.

CHAPTER NINE

Making Sure You're on Track

Spring cleaning! It dawns on you that it might be that time of year when you are looking for your lost keys in the sofa cushions and you find enough crusty old food to feed a family of four and enough loose change to buy a loaf of bread to go with it. All of a sudden you notice the dozen long-vacant cobwebs in the corners of the ceilings, the warning signs posted on your overfilled closets, and the dust bunnies mating under the bed. Yes, it's that time of year when you must put your pantry, closets, drawers, and *life* in order. Ah, springtime, you sigh as you put on the gloves; it is, after all, a time of renewal.

And renewing your commitment to your goals is something you ought to do periodically. Even if your spring-clean-a-thon consists only of dumping stale crackers out of the bottom of your purse or cleaning the lint out of your favorite jacket pockets, it's a good idea to take a look at your financial goals and the mutual funds you have chosen at least once a year to make sure you are still on track.

And the good news is that the process of monitoring the progress of your mutual funds is pretty much the same as the one you went through when you bought them.

Since it all began with you and your choices, we are going to take a look at the big picture you were looking at the day you finally made your choice and first opened your mutual fund account.

Here is a simple spring cleaning checklist that will help you take a quick inventory of where you were, where you are now, and where you are headed with each of your chosen mutual funds:

SPRING CLEANING CHECKLIST

1. Objective

2. Total return

3. Scorecard numbers

4. Comparative index

5. Other funds

The Chosen One's Objective

What was your financial objective when you first opened your mutual fund account? Is it still the same? If you started on a growth path, are you still striving to achieve the same long-term goals? If the answer is yes, place a check mark next to the word *objective* and move on.

But what if your objective has changed? What if you are within two years of your goal or within two to five years of retirement? In that case, I'll give you a sneak preview of this rule-of-thumb investment rebalancing chart on the next page.

This chart shows you how to rebalance the investments in your growth fund. You use the left side of the chart, entitled "Lump Sum Distribution from Your Investments," if you have the type of investments

ASSET ALLOCATION TABLE

Years away from goal date	Lump Sum Distribution from Your Investments				Income-Generating Investments			
	Portion of your total investment in each investment category				Portion of your total investment in each investment category			
	Stock Mutual Funds	Domestic Hybrid Funds	Bond Funds	Money Market Mutual Funds	Stock Mutual Funds	Domestic Hybrid Funds	Bond Funds	Money Market Mutual Funds
5	1/2	1/2	-0-	-0-	1/2	1/2	-0-	-0-
4	1/3	1/3	1/3	-0-	1/3	1/3	1/3	-0-
3*	-0-	1/3	2/3	Dividends and capital gains	1/3	1/3	1/3	Dividends and capital gains
2	-0-			T-bills and/or money market mutual funds	1/3	1/3	1/3	Any amount you wish to have readily accessible to you within two years**

* Open a money market mutual find account and begin receiving capital gains and dividend distributions in cash as a direct deposit into this account.

** Every year transfer monies from your mutual funds into your money market fund as needed. Always transfer money from the accounts that are showing the highest returns at the time into your money market fund.

that require a one-time cash out and not a monthly income from interest, such as a college fund. You use the right side, "Income-Generating Investments," if you would like to live off the interest of an investment such as a retirement nest egg or a lump-sum inheritance or a lottery winning.

We will cover this chart in detail and what to do if your objective has changed from growth to income, or from growth to mixed, and how to subsequently change your investment strategy in chapters 10 and 11.

But if you still have a growth objective, stay right where you are. Your fund's got some 'splainin' to do.

The Chosen One's Performance

How has your fund performed? To get an answer to this question, you need to calculate the fund's *total return*. We'll use a handy chart to track your mutual fund's performance, which you can print out from www.JulieStav. com; I suggest that you date this chart in your investment notebook so you can compare your results next year, too. Take out your calculator and:

1. Punch in the number of shares you own in the fund and multiply this times the most recent price per share (NAV). To get the most recent price per share, go to www.finance.yahoo.com. Type in the symbol for your fund in the box, and click "GO." You will see the NAV of your fund. For example, if you own 150 shares, and the net asset value per share was twenty dollars, your result would be:

   150 shares × $20 per share = $3,000 ending balance

   Write this number down next to step 1:

   STEP 1: Ending balance (shares × price per share) $3,000

   STEP 2: Total deposits for the year

   STEP 3: Profit (step 2 − step 1)

   STEP 4: Percent profit of deposit (profit ÷ deposits)

   STEP 5: Total return for the year (step 4 × 100)

   STEP 6: Total annualized return (step 5 ÷ yrs in)

2. Figure out the amount you have deposited during the year. For example, if you deposited $200 per month, your total deposits for the year would be:

$200 per month × 12 months = $2,400 deposited

This is what to write in step 2:

STEP 1: Ending balance (shares × price per share) $3,000

STEP 2: Total deposits for the year $2,400

STEP 3: Profit (step 2 − step 1)

STEP 4: Percent profit of deposit (profit ÷ deposits)

STEP 5: Total return for the year (step 4 × 100)

STEP 6: Total annualized return (step 5 ÷ yrs in)

3. Now subtract the total you invested (step 2) from the value of your account (step 1). The difference will be the profits you have for the year. This step should look like this:

$3,000 − $2,400 = $600 profit

STEP 1: Ending balance (shares × price per share) $3,000

STEP 2: Total deposits for the year $2,400

STEP 3: Profit (step 2 − step 1) $600

STEP 4: Percent profit of deposit (profit ÷ deposits)

STEP 5: Total return for the year (step 4 × 100)

STEP 6: Total annualized return (step 5 ÷ yrs in)

4. Next we need to find out what percentage this profit is of the amount you deposited into this account. Divide your profit amount by the amount you deposited throughout the year like this:

$$\$600 \text{ profits} \div \$2,400 = .25$$

Fill in step 4 with this amount:

STEP 1: Ending balance (shares × price per share) $3,000

STEP 2: Total deposits for the year $2,400

STEP 3: Profit (step 2 − step 1) $600

STEP 4: Percent profit of deposit (profit ÷ deposits) 0.25

STEP 5: Total return for the year (step 4 × 100)

STEP 6: Total annualized return (step 5 ÷ yrs in)

5. Multiply this number times 100 to get to its percent. The result will be your *total return* for the year.

$$.25 \times 100 = 25\%$$

This is what your tally should look like now:

STEP 1: Ending balance (shares × price per share) $3,000

STEP 2: Total deposits for the year $2,400

STEP 3: Profit (step 2 − step 1) $600

STEP 4: Percent profit of deposit (profit ÷ deposits) 0.25

STEP 5: Total return for the year (step 4 × 100) 25 percent

STEP 6: Total annualized return (step 5 ÷ yrs in)

The previous example shows a gain of 25 percent for the year. Therefore, your total return is 25 percent for one year.

6. If you have been investing in your mutual fund longer than one year, divide your result in step 5 by the number of years you have been investing. This is how you will get an average annual return for your mutual fund. For example, if you have invested in this fund for three years, even if you have deposited different monthly amounts during this period, divide 25 percent by three:

.25 ÷ 3 years = 8.33%

STEP 1: Ending balance (shares × price per share) $3,000

STEP 2: Total deposits for the year $2,400

STEP 3: Profit (step 2 − step 1) $600

STEP 4: Percent profit of deposit (profit ÷ deposits) 0.25

STEP 5: Total return for the year (step 4 × 100) 25%

STEP 6: Total annualized return (step 5 ÷ yrs in) 8%

It is possible that when you multiplied the number of shares you own times the current share value and figured out your profit, you ended up with a negative number; regardless, proceed through the aforementioned steps anyway. The end result will be a negative percent, meaning that your account lost value. Don't despair. Remember: *You are in it for the long haul, and all mutual funds go through their ups and downs at one time or another.* Although it feels like a punch to the stomach, this is an inevitable phase in mutual fund investing. Take a deep breath and move on.

If your fund didn't go up in value, or if it went up just a little bit, don't judge your fund before at least three years' time has passed. It's too early. You are still years from your goal, and you must give that mutual fund an opportunity to go through the normal ups and downs every fund goes through. This is the reason you invested only money you would not need to have access to for at least two years into this mutual fund. It takes time for money to make money. So hold on.

If, however, you have been in the fund for a three-year period, and for the past three to five years the total return has been far lower than other funds in the same category, then hold on to your hats. We'll soon discuss some alternatives.

Run the Numbers on Your Fund

Take out the same blank mutual fund candidates scorecard you used to evaluate your fund purchase in chapter 8 and look up your fund as if you were investing in it for the first time by going to www.morningstar.com. Type in the ticker symbol for your particular mutual fund in the box at the top of the page. If you do not know the ticker symbol, type in the name of the fund and the search function on the site should pop up with a helpful fund name list.

To remind you what it looks like, on page 140 is another blank fund candidates scorecard which you can also print out from www.JulieStav.com.

Use the numbers you find in the report to fill in your scorecard. You will record the total return (remember that the total return stated in the report may refer to a different annual time period from your own, so calculate your own total return using the steps on pages 119–25, the fees imposed by the fund, the beta score, and the Bear Market Decile Rank, if available. How does it all look when you compare it to the original scoreboard when you bought the fund? Again, remember to expect fluctuations in performance when looking at the short-term (one-year) return.

If it looks like you are still on target, good for you. If not, we'll cover your options in a few pages.

Check Out the Index Mirrored by Your Fund

Write down the best-fit index for your fund. You will find this information in the "beta" section of the Morningstar Quicktake® Report. (Click on the "Risk Measures" heading in the left-hand navigational bar.)

FUND CANDIDATES SCORECARD

Fund Name	Total Return						Beta		Fees				Bear Market Decile Rank
	1-Yr Return	Net 1-Yr Return*	3-Yr Return	5-Yr Return	3-Yr % Rank	Cat. Rating	Vs. S&P 500	Vs. Best Fit Index	Front-end	Back-end	Expense Ratio	12 (b)1	

*The Net 1-Year Return represents the one-year return minus any front-end or back-end fees. Morningstar's 1-Year Return figures already reflect the Expense Ratio and 12(b)1 fee, so we don't need to subtract them again.

Write the name of the appropriate index on your score sheet as if it were another fund. Go to www.indexfunds.com. In the search window of the "Data Central" option, click on "Indexes." Check the boxes next to the capitalization and style of your fund (e.g., "MidCap" and "Growth"), making sure to remove the check from the box next to "All Indexes." In the "Sort By" box, make sure it says "Index Name," and then click on the "Screen!" button. Scroll down the alphabetized list of indexes until you find your best-fit index. Write down the average annual returns of the index for one, three, and five years. By doing this, you will see how your fund compares to the index that represents the holdings of your fund. Does the return of your fund match or surpass that of its index? We want this answer to be *yes*!

If the answer is a resounding no for the past three to five years, then this is a confirmation that your fund may be losing steam. Hang on, we have some solutions coming up.

Check with the Joneses

Do you remember how you found other funds within the same investment size and style on the Morningstar site? You want to do this again to see how other funds that invest in the same type of stocks or bonds as your fund are doing so you can compare results.

Go to www.morningstar.com and click on the "Mutual Fund Screener" option. Under "Fund Type" click on the drop-down window next to "Morningstar Category" and choose the capitalization and style that describes your fund (i.e., mid-value, large growth, etc.). Click "Show Results." View the list by "Performance" and click on the 3-year return (%) heading. Take a look at other funds that have the same capitalization and investment style as yours. Note the three-, six-, and ten-year returns. Are there funds that have consistently performed better than yours? If so, check out the beta and category rating of those funds. Are they taking more or less risk with their investors' money than your fund is?

What is important here is the frequency with which other funds surpass your fund's returns. If you see repeatedly that fund X outperforms your particular fund over the past twelve months, three years, *and* five years with *less* risk as measured by its beta, that might be an indication that fund X merits further study.

Even though it may be tempting to switch accounts when you see that some other fund is thriving while yours seems to be in hibernation, resist the temptation to fund-hop. If you made a decision to open an account with your mutual fund based on solid findings, you need to develop a thick skin for those possible flash-in-the-pan funds that may shine for only a short term. Read your fund's prospectus again. Look back at your initial fund candidate scorecard.

Rereading the prospectus may seem redundant at this point, but it is a good idea to refresh your mind regarding what the mutual fund's objective is and what your own is now. Don't be surprised if you find some interesting reading in this rather cumbersome document. The more familiar you become with the workings of your funds, the more meaningful details you will remember about it. Read about your fund's risk and what the managers are planning to do to generate profits. Perhaps the fund is starting to engage in risky transactions. That might be a red flag for you, indicating that it's time to move on.

You will get a very good sense of your mutual fund's progress by going through this reacquaintance process each year. The benefits of this practice extend beyond reconfirming your initial investment decision. This practice also introduces you to other possible investment opportunities you may have overlooked or new ones that may have entered the market and might be worth some study.

Once you have reviewed your mutual fund performance and restated your goals, you will feel more connected to your investments. Over time, you will feel accomplished. You are making things happen through hard work, discipline, and persistence. That is the secret of successful investing!

But what do you do if three or more of the five spring cleaning benchmarks point to your fund's being a real, live stinker? Hold your nose, the answer is in this next section.

When to Move on Out

If your fund's total returns are lagging for a period of three years, go through the process of looking at your options with a fresh outlook.

Go to www.indexfunds.com and check out the three-year performance of the indexes again.[1] If you are invested in mid-caps, do you still see them show up on your list among the first five funds? If your fund's style is value, is value a popular contender in these top five indexes? If the answer is no, make a note of those that are in the lead, and follow the same process of elimination as you did when you originally invested in this gone-sour mutual fund. What you'll need to do at this point if your objective has stayed the same is go back to chapter 8 and reinvestigate funds starting from scratch using a blank scorecard. Then compare your initial fund candidates scorecard with the new one.

If the total returns are better in a new fund while the beta rating is the same or perhaps even lower, it is time to seriously consider a legal separation from your initial choice. You may opt to stop investing in the first fund and open a second one or sell the first fund and reinvest the money in the new choice. Note that if you do make that move outside your retirement program, selling your first fund will have tax consequences. Consult with your tax accountant before making this decision since he/she may suggest you do it during a specific time of the year to minimize the effect of taxes on your general financial picture.

[1] To figure out which indexes are on top, go to www.indexfunds.com. Scroll down to "Data Central." Make sure that "Indexes" is showing in the drop-down window and click on the "Go" button. Click on the boxes next to "Large Cap," "Mid Cap," and "Small Cap," creating a check in each. In the drop-down window next to "Sort by" choose "3-Year Returns." Do not do anything else. Move down to the "Screen" button and click. (If you want to see funds in only one capitalization size, put a check only in that box and not the other two.)

Run That by Me Again?

To reiterate, here is the spring cleaning checklist you need to use every year:

1. *Check objective: growth or income?* If it hasn't changed from your previous year's objective, go to the next steps. If your objective has changed from growth to income, skip to chapter 10.

2. *Calculate total return.* Use the six-step chart shown on pages 135–38. Is your total return higher or lower than last year's total return? If you have been investing in the fund for only one year, don't make a decision to change yet. Wait until you have been in it for at least three years before deciding to kiss a fund good-bye.

3. *Run the numbers again using the fund candidates scorecard.* Go to www.morningstar.com and check out your fund's vital signs by checking out the following:

    a. Total return. Remember that these are the total returns that are published in the mutual fund reports, and they may represent different starting and closing dates than yours; thus, the reported return may be different than your results in step 2. For example, you may have looked at the total return on your individual account from August to August, while the fund reports are showing the results from May to May.

    b. Fees

    c. Beta

    d. Bear Market Decile Rank (if any)

    What you want to ask here is: How has my fund performed when compared to last year's report? Is the total return up, or are we going through a downtrend? Are the fees higher or lower than last year's fees? Has the fund taken on more risk and volatility than it previously did? Has the Bear Market Decile Rank changed? Again, don't judge it until you have been in it for at least three years.

4. *Check the index that mirrors your fund.* Go to www.indexfunds.com. In the "Indexes" section you can find out if your fund's one-, three-, and five-year returns match or surpass the index's. If the answer is yes, that it matches or surpasses, you are still going strong. If your fund seems to be falling behind its representative index *over those three time periods*, pay close attention to the next step to see who the new leaders may be.

5. *Check out the Joneses.* Go to www.morningstar.com and use the "Mutual Fund Screener" to determine how similar funds are doing. Two questions to ask here: Are their total (one-, three-, and five-year) returns and beta ratings higher or lower than your fund's? Are they assuming more or less risk than your fund is? If you see that after three years or so, a fund other than your own comes out ahead over and over again, you may consider this new fund as your prime candidate, and a change in your fund holdings may be in order.

Now that you know how to check where you were and where you are now to see if it still matches where you are going, what do you do if your objective has changed? Read on. In chapter 10 we are going to address what to do if you need some money—fast.

CHAPTER TEN

Gearing Up to Gear Down

I imagine by now that if you have put into practice the system you learned in this book, you are patting yourself so hard on the back you're almost breaking your arm. As well you should!

You managed to keep your end of the bargain and religiously invested every month into your mutual fund account. Up to now, your investment objective was growth. You were interested in the future value of your account rather than in receiving income, and you knew that stock-based mutual funds, over time, consistently outperformed any other type of investment. You have been investing for years now, and you have endured trying moments in the stock market when it was mighty tempting to stop throwing money into what at times seemed like a sinking ship. But you persevered, and in spite of the inevitable storms along the way, you stuck it out, knowing that the only way to win in the mutual fund game was by not being a fair-weather friend.

Yes, the rewards of taking control of your financial life by making a good, solid investment and watching it grow are incredibly empowering, not to mention lucrative.

But there comes a time when you are finally closer to your financial goal. Once that time comes, and you are two to five years from your goal, your objective necessarily changes. Where you once had a growth objective because you needed your money to grow as fast as possible, you now have a mixed growth and income objective: You need to start gathering income now or soon, or you need to protect the lump sum of money that you have to cash out soon. Or maybe you've just received a large chunk of change (you'll miss Uncle Albert, but the millions he left you will enable you to retire in style) and you want to invest that money so that it can start generating income immediately.

Whichever the case may be, it's time to remap your flight plan.

Your Objective Is Income: Now or Within Two to Five Years

Who falls into this group? Medium- or long-term investors within five years of their goal, such as those investing toward a retirement nest egg or a lump-sum college or wedding fund; investors who have come into a substantial lump sum and want to live off their interest; and short-term investors who will now need the money within two years.

Each of the investors who belong in this group share a need to learn about more conservative kinds of mutual funds. Whether transitioning to income or going straight to income, you need to learn how to allocate or reallocate the funds in your investment portfolio. In plain English, that means that instead of investing in mutual funds that are on the safest fast track toward the highest possible profits, you need to invest in more of a mix of fast trackers and slower trackers and maybe even some real snail's-pace trackers.

This process is the same one we take when we approach a stop sign on the road. We anticipate its proximity and begin to slow down as we get closer to it. You can't expect to go from sixty-five to zero miles per hour in one fell swoop . . . not without risking whiplash, anyway. In investment lingo, this transition is called *reallocating*. And before you can do that, you need to learn about the more conservative, *income-producing* mutual fund choices at your disposal.

There are numerous income-generating funds from which to choose, but we will concentrate on a few that will offer you the ability to gear down to a slower speed when approaching your financial goal.[1]

Shock-Absorbing Funds

Sports cars are known for their speed and their quick response to road conditions. When you start up one of those beauties, you buckle up and get ready to experience the ride. Every curve and bump is accentuated as you feel your mechanical beast take on the challenge of the road ahead. Luxury cars, on the other hand, pride themselves in a ride so smooth that at sixty miles an hour, if you believe their advertising, you can pour champagne into a tall glass while sitting perched on the hood of the car and not spill a drop!

Which is all to say that the ride with stock funds is equal to that in a Porsche, while these income-generating options provide a ride more like a Lincoln Town Car's, since they tend to counteract the volatility of the stock market and smooth out its bumps better than stock funds.

Because of that, the following choices may not be able to compete in the total return arena, but they do offer soothing relief in the beta department—relief that may let you sleep much better at night as you get closer to your financial goal and start seeing dollar signs in your sleep.

Bond Funds

You may impress your family at the dinner table by quoting your stock fund's capitalization or investment style, but it's rather unlikely that they

---

[1] Some of you might be saying right now, "But I am an aggressive investor with a strong stomach for volatility. I am willing to ride the ups and downs of the market until the day I retire." That's nice for you, but have you ever considered what will happen if the market turns nasty the day before you want to retire? You might be forced to sell something at a loss in order to get the income you need to live on. Since we are *not* in this to lose money, and since we want to avoid this ugly scenario, we start to transition and reallocate our funds within five years of our goal.

will stop shoveling in the meat loaf when they hear you mention your bond's duration or quality. Bonds are just not glamorous creatures.

However, bond mutual funds may offer added stability when sprinkled into your investment choices as you get closer to your goal.

What are bond funds? They are those mutual funds that lend rather than invest their money. "Whaddya mean, exactly?" you say, perplexed. What I mean is that bond funds collect money from investors and then loan these monies out. When they loan money to companies, they are called *corporate bonds*. When they loan money to the government, they are called *government bonds*.

Historically, bond funds have trailed the returns of their glitzier relatives, the stock funds; however, bond funds offer an oasis during those times when the stock market goes through corrections. Since we don't know how long these corrections may last, bond funds may soften the blow of market downtrends.

Bond investors do not share directly in the benefits of a company's growth. You, as a bond fund investor (or bond holder), have lent money to a corporation, and as a lender, you will earn interest on your money. In the meantime, if the company is successful and the price of its shares goes up, the value of your bond does *not* grow along with that share price. However, while stock investors wait in the hopes of collecting a higher price for their shares at some point in the future, you are already regularly receiving periodic payments from your bonds. You are giving up on sharing the potential future profits in lieu of some money now. That's the way it works.

Remember how we used the S&P 500 Index as the benchmark for measuring the returns of the stock market in the United States? Well, bond funds also have representation, and there is an index for bonds as well: the Lehman Brothers Bond Indexes. These indexes track the growth of bonds in different categories.

Here is a picture of how corporate and bond funds have fared over the past fifteen years when compared to stock funds. As you can see, the ups and downs of the stock market are like peaks and valleys along the top line, while the two parallel lines in the middle—those that belong to the corporate and government bonds—show a smoother journey. Such is the life of a bond. No fireworks, but no deep depressions, either.

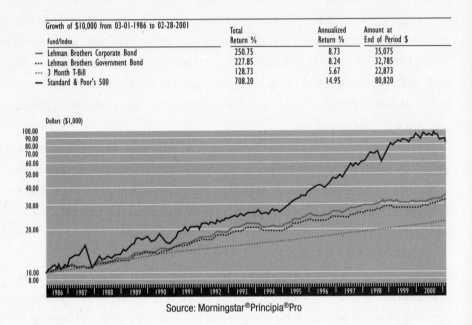

Growth of $10,000 from 03-01-1986 to 02-28-2001	Total	Annualized	Amount at
Fund/Index	Return %	Return %	End of Period $
— Lehman Brothers Corporate Bond	250.75	8.73	35,075
··· Lehman Brothers Government Bond	227.85	8.24	32,785
··· 3 Month T-Bill	128.73	5.67	22,873
— Standard & Poor's 500	708.20	14.95	80,820

Source: Morningstar®Principia®Pro

A bond fund may or may not be taxable. Corporate and government bonds are generally taxable, which means that both the dividends paid (if any) and the capital gains (if any) are subject to federal, state, and local taxes. On the other hand, with municipal bonds, which are issued by state and local government entities, the interest earned is generally exempt from federal income taxes and in some cases also from state and local taxes.

Characteristics of Bonds

Every bond has a maturity date, which simply refers to the time when the original amount the investor or the mutual fund lent the company is returned. If you invest in a bond directly, you are lending the money to the company, you receive interest while the loan is outstanding, and you receive the loaned amount at the end of the term. When you invest in a bond fund, the mutual fund company is the one that is lending the money to the corporation or government body, the one that receives interest, and the one that gets the money back at the end of the loan period. The interest and profits (or losses) are passed on to you as the investor of the fund, but you don't have to worry about the maturity date of each bond since you are investing in them indirectly, through your mutual fund company. You own shares of the fund; you don't own the bonds directly.

Every bond also has a coupon rate, which is the dividend (or interest) that the company pays the lender during the loan period. Again, if you bought a bond directly, you would be the recipient of the interest along the way; if you invest in bonds through a mutual fund company, it is the fund that receives the interest payments and then passes them on to you as the investor in the fund.

When a mutual fund invests in bonds, it holds many different bonds from different entities with different maturity dates and coupon rates. Since you are investing in the mutual fund company and not buying the bonds themselves, you don't have to deal with maturity dates or interest payments. Your money comes from the fund, not from the bonds directly. Mutual fund companies publish the *average* maturity date and *average* coupon rates of all the bonds they own in their mutual fund reports. These two averages provide the information we use to evaluate them.

Performance: How to Judge Bond Funds

There are two factors that affect the performance of bonds: *duration* and *credit quality*. Duration reflects how long the companies in the fund have to pay back their loans, and credit quality refers to the ability of that company to handle and repay the loan.

First let's talk about a bond's duration and how it affects the bond's price. According to Morningstar, Inc., duration comes in three flavors in taxable bonds: short-term duration (in which the term of the loans in the fund averages less than 3.5 years), intermediate-term duration (averages 3.5 to 6 years), and long-term duration (averages longer than 6 years).

The longer a bond's duration period, the longer the companies can take to pay back the money they owe the fund. The more time that passes between the time the loan is taken out and the time the loan has to be paid back, the more of a chance that interest rates may go up or down. And interest rates directly affect the price of the bond. Bond prices, just like stock prices, can go up or down.

Rising interest rates are a bond price's worst enemy, since they *inversely* affect a bond's price or *value*. That means that when interest rates go up, the value of your funds will go down; when interest rates go down, the value of your funds will go up.

According to Morningstar, Inc., a good rule of thumb is that if a bond fund has a duration of five years, you can expect it to gain 5 percent if interest rates *fall* by one percentage point; and you can also expect it to lose 5 percent if interest rates *rise* by one percentage point. So a bond fund with a duration period of four years should be twice as volatile as a bond fund with a duration of two years.

All this is to say that the longer the duration of each bond in a bond fund, the higher the risk that maybe the debt won't get paid back on time or in full and the more chance interest rates have to dance up or down, which in turn means the more chance the price of the bond might fluctuate greatly.

Because of this reverse reaction to interest rates, and the fact that the longer the maturity date is the more chances for interest rates to fluctuate, *it makes more sense at this stage of the game for us to invest in bond funds that buy short duration bonds, from three to five years*. You are approaching D-day when you are going to cash in on your bond funds—and the less volatility the better.

Always check the mutual fund report for the duration of the bonds they hold. The shorter the duration, the less volatile the bond prices will be, and the fewer possible instances your fund manager might have in which he has to sell bonds at a discount to generate cash for the fund.

Now let's talk about credit quality. This has to do with the ability of the bond issuing company to repay the loan. If your brother-in-law was unemployed, didn't hold a job for five years, and asked you for a loan, you would probably think twice before handing over the money. But if your reliable, trustworthy, long-employed sister asked for a loan to cover a short-term emergency, you might be more willing to part with the funds to tide her over. The same concept applies to bonds: Those companies with a solid track record have a better rating than those that have fallen on hard times or are too new to rate.

How do you determine the financial well-being of companies that offer bonds? By looking to the firms that rate the quality of each company and its ability to repay its debt.

Two of the most popular credit rating firms are Moody's and Standard & Poor's. These firms take a very close look at a company's financial statement to determine its ability to pay back its bondholders. After carefully reviewing all the numbers, bonds are given a letter rating: AAA being the highest possible rating and D the lowest.

Bonds with ratings such as AAA, AA, A (in descending order), and BBB show a very good chance that the principal and dividend payments will be paid by the corporation that issued the bonds, whether they owe the money directly to you as an individual investor or to the mutual fund in which you invested. These preferred bonds are considered to be of *investment grade*. Anything rated BB, B, CCC, CC, or C (in descending order) is not considered investment grade. These bonds are called *junk bonds*. A bond rated D is usually already in default on its loans. Urgh!

Why would anyone in his/her right mind invest in a lower-rated bond? Because these bonds offer higher dividend payments to attract investors. Many investors are willing to take higher risks by investing in lower-rated bonds in order to collect higher dividends. Think of it like this: You know in the movies when the loan-shark mobsters buy the poor schlemiel's outstanding debt and then allow him to take longer to pay it back, but in exchange force him to pay it back at ten times what the original amount was? That's kind of like what junk bonds are. If you hold the original loan and you get paid back, you can make a lot of money. On the other hand, the schlemiel might keel over from a heart attack from all the anxiety of having to deal with the mob and then the mob is SOL (surely outta luck).

This is the reason why you must always check the quality of the bonds in your mutual fund. Don't be blindsided by the apparently high dividends the bond pays out. You just might end up holding an IOU not worth the paper it's printed on.

One Last Player in the Game

Before we go through the process of evaluating bond mutual funds, we are going to look at one more type of conservative, income-generating type of fund: *hybrid funds*.

No, these funds are not part of a bizarre scientific experiment. Hybrid funds are those that invest in stocks, bonds, and convertible bonds. "Please, just twirl it a bit more. Yeah, that's it. Make my head spin," you complain.

OK, one at a time. Investing in stocks you know about. Investing in bonds you know about. But what the heck are convertible bonds? All you need to know is that convertible bonds are those with an identity crisis. Even though they are born bonds, these fellows can, at some point, stop being bonds and be traded for stocks at a prearranged price. Convertible bond investors feel it's like having your cake and eating it, too. They receive interest payments from the bonds and, at some point in the future, they can decide to convert those bonds into stocks. These investors need to know if and when it makes sense to make a conversion to a stock. This is when, once again, mutual fund managers earn their keep, since they make all those day-to-day decisions on behalf of the fund investors.

Why do hybrid funds exist? Because by investing in stocks *and* bonds *and* convertible bonds, hybrid mutual funds aim to preserve the ability to show growth over time while providing current income. In other words, by juggling all these types of investments in one fund, they can pay some money out while still growing a bit faster than most conservative bond funds. They are thus great transitional investments.

Hybrid funds can come in the form of *balanced funds* (those that try to keep a balance between stocks and bonds), or *income funds* (which attempt to provide income by concentrating in either bonds or the dividends that their stocks may generate).

OK, enough of this. Let's figure out the meat and potatoes of bond and hybrid funds. First, we will learn how to evaluate bond funds on-line.[2] Evaluating hybrid funds come in a bit later in this chapter.

Where's the Beef?

As you learned in chapter 7, the starting point for any mutual fund evaluation begins with its *total return*. After all, generating profits is the reason for investing in the first place. Total return represents the profit that is being generated as a result of buying and selling securities (whether stocks or bonds).

Go to www.morningstar.com. Click on the "Mutual Fund Screener" option.

In the middle of the screen in the "Fund Type" window, you will see "Morningstar Category." Since short-term bonds are considered more attractive to conservative investors, we will go with them. So open the drop-down window on "Morningstar Category" and choose "Short-Term Bond." Your screen should look like this:

---

[2] You can also find all this on-line information in Morningstar Quicktake® Reports at the library.

Set Criteria

Fund Type　　　🔍 Fund group:　　　　　　　　　　　| All ⬍ |

　　　　　　　　🔍 Morningstar Category:　　　　　　| Short-Term Bond ⬍ |

　　　　　　　　🔍 Manager tenure greater than or equal to:　| Any ⬍ |
　　　　　　　　　　　　　Source: www.morningstar.com

Then scroll down past the "Cost and Purchase" section to the "Ratings and Risk" section of your screen, and open the small window in the section of "Category risk better than or equal to." Choose "Below Average" in the drop-down window. Your screen should now look like this:

Ratings and Risk　　Check all the ratings that you would like to include:

　　　　　　　　🔍 Morningstar Star Rating
　　　　　　　　☐ ★
　　　　　　　　☐ ★★
　　　　　　　　☐ ★★★
　　　　　　　　☐ ★★★★
　　　　　　　　☐ ★★★★★
　　　　　　　　☐ New, unrated funds

　　　　　　　　🔍 Morningstar Risk better than or equal to:　| Below Average ⬍ |
　　　　　　　　　　　　　Source: www.morningstar.com

What you have done so far is request to be shown all the short-term bond funds, whether government or corporate, that fall into a below average–risk category as measured by Morningstar, Inc.

We have one more criterion that we can designate on this screen. All this initial work is worth it, because it will save us having to peruse through many bond funds that do not merit our consideration. We are searching for the crème de la crème here, and the more restrictions we can impose, the better qualified our choices will be.

Scroll to the bottom of the screen. In the "Portfolio" section, you will see a small area with the subheading "For bond funds." In this area, we get to choose the "Average credit quality" of our mutual fund, that is, the ability of the companies to repay their debt. As we discussed, we want only the funds with great credit, so let's choose "A or higher" in our drop-down window. This choice will restrict the program to come up only with those mutual funds that lend money to corporations or government bodies with a credit rating of A or better.

Again we need to reiterate our wish to see short-term duration bond funds, so let's choose "less than or = to 5 years" in the "Duration" drop-down window.

This is what your screen looks like now:

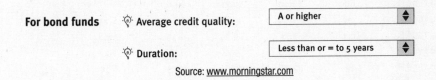

Source: www.morningstar.com

That's it for now. Go down to the bottom of the screen and click on the "Show Results" button, then sit back and watch the list of eager candidates parade onto your screen.

Since there is a pretty good possibility that you are going to be given lines and lines of funds to consider, let's sort them by performance before continuing. Can you believe our good fortune? We can be really picky here to get exactly what we want!

Do you see a light blue area on the left-hand side of your screen? Under the tab that says "Change Criteria" there is a drop-down window next to the word "View," with the word "Snapshot" showing. Open that drop-down window and choose "Performance" to line up our ducks by how well they are doing.

Once your list has come up on your screen, in the column headings find and double-click on the heading "3-year Return (%)." Clicking on this will result in all the mutual funds scurrying to show themselves to you, arranged from the best of them to the worst of them as determined by their three-year total return. (As with other mutual funds, bond funds are best judged by their three-year returns.)

Take a look at the list I got on April 26, 2001, by following the directions I have outlined so far in this chapter. I have made up the fund names to keep everyone focused on the numbers, not the names. *Remember, your results will be different from what you see here.*

Fund Name	Category Risk	YTD Return (%)	1–Year Return (%)	3–Year Return (%)	5–Year Return (%)	10–Year Return (%)
Bond Fund A	Low	2.70	9.77	6.79	--	--
Bond Fund B	Low	3.10	9.73	6.68	6.59	--
Bond Fund C	Low	3.39	9.93	6.51	6.25	--
Bond Fund D	Low	3.40	10.31	6.50	--	--
Bond Fund E	Low	3.44	9.88	6.44	6.23	--
Bond Fund F	Low	2.75	9.35	6.39	6.48	6.18
Bond Fund G	Low	3.00	9.40	6.36	6.27	--
Bond Fund H	Low	2.25	8.51	6.23	6.10	--
Bond Fund I	Low	2.68	7.15	6.10	6.19	--
Bond Fund J	Low	2.46	8.08	6.07	6.35	--

Source: www.morningstar.com

Wow! Here is the list of the best candidates that meet our criteria. These mutual funds are the best-performing short-term bond funds with a five-year or less duration period, a low risk category, and an average credit rating of A or better.

Take a moment to look over this list. You can see that there is only one mutual fund among these finalists that shows returns over a ten-year period. The reason for this is that it's the only candidate that has been around that long. I like to see a mutual fund that has been around for a long period of time. Stability is important here. Again, since you are closer to your end goal and will need access to this money soon, you simply can't be worrying about your fund's volatility. That money better be available for you when you need it. As such, this fund's longevity is a good thing.

Your Bond Squad

Just so we can keep our numbers straight, let's use another scorecard which you can see on the next page. This time we will call it our bond squad scorecard; it's for you to keep track of the most important factors to consider when evaluating a bond mutual fund. Make a photocopy of the chart on page 160, or draw it in your notebook. It's also available for printing out at www.JulieStav.com.

Seniority Counts

Limit your candidates to a manageable number by choosing the top four funds from the initial list on your screen.

Which ones do you choose? First, look for the one with the longest track record of *stable* returns. Disregard the one-year return, since the past twelve months represent a very short period of time in the life of mutual funds, and a bond fund is a type of mutual fund, so we shouldn't base our investment decisions on this short performance. Let's consider the average track record instead; that way, the temporary highs and lows will be smoothed out, and we can see the true trend of the fund's performance.

For example, if the fund returned an average of 11 percent over the past three-year period, 2 percent during the last five years, and 8 percent over the last ten, I would not consider that to be a stable record of return.

If, however, you have the scenario we can see on Bond Fund F above, where the average returns of the fund for the past three, five, and ten years are 6.39 percent, 6.48 percent, and 6.18 percent, respectively, you can readily see that these returns are all within half of a percent from each other. That's a very stable return over a long period of time. The rule of thumb here regarding stability is: *The closer the three-, five-, and ten-year total return numbers are to one another, the better.*

Write this fund first on your bond squad scorecard. Fill in the numbers for the three-, five-, and ten-year returns.

BOND SQUAD SCORECARD

| Fund Name | Total Return | | | | | | Fees | | | | Beta | Avg. Credit Rating | Avg. Duration |
	1-Yr Return	Net 1-Yr Return*	3-Yr Return	5-Yr Return	10-Yr Return	Yield	Front-end	Back-end	Expense Ratio	12 (b)1			

*The Net 1-Year Return represents the one-year return minus any front-end or back-end fees. Morningstar's 1-Year Return figures already reflect the Expense Ratio and 12(b)1 fee, so we don't need to subtract them again.

Then, in order to be able to take a look at the mutual fund Quick-take® Report from Morningstar, click on the name of your first chosen fund. You now will be looking at your fund's report.

What's Really in It for You?

You have already filled in the respective total returns of your first fund. In a bond fund, however, it is important to note not only the total return of the fund but also its *yield;* that is, the interest rate that the bond fund is currently paying its shareholders over a twelve-month period. *The most important thing to remember is that the yield must be lower than the one-year total return of the fund.* Here is why.

Let's pretend that you have to pay a daily parking fee for a part-time job you hold in a busy section of the city. You are getting paid ten dollars a day for the one hour of work you do there each day, and your parking fee is twelve dollars. *Gong!* Something is wrong there! It won't take you very long to see that you are not really getting paid for this job; in fact, you are paying two dollars a day for the privilege of working there! Bogus.

The same scenario occurs when you have a mutual fund that is offering a higher interest rate (or yield) to its shareholders than the total return of the fund. They are paying out more money than is coming in. That ought to set off some alarms. Something has to give, and what usually gives is the share value of that fund: The price of the shares is actually *decreasing* in value because the mutual fund is dipping into it to make up the difference between the interest it's paying out and the profit it is generating. That mutual fund is in essence eating itself up to be able to keep up with those high interest payments. Totally bogus.

Who would put up with that kind of crazy math? Well, many bond mutual fund investors only look at the yields they are receiving in the form of income from their mutual funds and fail to look at the total return or the diminishing price of their shares. This sad practice results in a gradual erosion of their accounts. You can see these investors walking down the street with satisfied smiles on their faces because they feel safe and secure while receiving their monthly dividend checks. Little do they know that they are cannibalizing their account to produce those high returns! What they should really be looking at is the share price part on their monthly statement: If the share price is slowly eroding over time, when you go to sell your shares, you will sell at such a loss that all those paid-out dividends won't make up for your losses.

So take a look at the total return versus the yield and make sure that your fund is not paying out more than it's bringing in. Rule of thumb: *The yield must be lower than the total return to make it worth your while.*

To find a fund's current yield, go down the left navigational bar until you reach the "Portfolio" heading. Under that, click on the "Top 25 Holdings" choice on the left-hand side of your screen.

It should look something like this:

Top 25 Holdings Get Price Quotes			
Total number of stock holdings	0	Turnover %	4
Total number of bond holdings	8	Yield %	4.6 ←
% Assets in top 10 holdings	27.5		

Source: www.morningstar.com

Record the yield on your scorecard, and compare it to the total return for one year. (The only reason we are looking at one-year returns here is for the sake of comparison: Yield is based on twelve months. Apples to apples.) In the case of Mutual Bond Fund F, the one-year total return is 9.35 percent. The chart above shows us that the yield for the previous twelve months was 4.6 percent.

If you subtract 4.6 percent (the fund's yield) from its total one-year return of 9.35 percent, you are still left with 4.75 percent, which represents the growth of this mutual fund even after paying out its interest. This is a good thing.

How Much Is that Doggie in the Window?

Next, check on your fund's fees. As with other mutual funds, this is an important factor to consider, but it's especially important when investing in a bond mutual fund. Since the returns of bond funds are usually lower than those of stocks, there is actually *less* money from which to pay expenses. A bond fund that knows how to keep its expenses low will end up keeping more profits for its investors.

Click on the "Fees and Expenses" option in the Morningstar.com navigational bar at the left of your screen.

Look for front-end and back-end expenses, as well as the 12(b)1 fees and total expense ratios. *All expenses, including the 12(b)1 fees, are reflected on the total return figures on Morningstar.com.* Put this information in your bond squad scorecard in the appropriate places.

As you can see in the following chart, this fund does not have any front- or back-end fees, and the total expense ratio is .56 percent.

Fees and Expenses

Maximum Sales Fees		Total Cost Projections (per $10,000)	
Initial	None	3-Year	$268
Deferred	None	5-Year	$466
Redemption	None	10-Year	$1037
Maximum Fees		**Actual Fees**	
Administrative	0.00%	12(b)1	0.00%
Management	0.40%	Management	0.40%
12b-1	0.00%	Total Expense Ratio	0.56%

Source: www.morningstar.com

How Well Will It Let You Sleep at Night?

As you learned in chapter 7, beta is the measurement you use to gauge the volatility or risk of a mutual fund. Click on "Risk Measures" on the left navigational bar to check out this fund's beta rating. Here's how Bond Fund F's beta looked:

	Standard Index LB Aggregate	Best Fit Index Lehman Brothers Aggregate Bond
R-Squared	78	78
Beta ⟶	0.38	0.38
Alpha	0.49	0.49

Source: www.morningstar.com

Notice that the rating for beta under best-fit index is 0.38 percent, which means that this fund has less than half the volatility of the index that represents it. This is a sign of a very stable fund. The rule of thumb here is: *In a short-term bond fund, any beta that is lower than .50 percent is considered a low beta.*[3] Fill in this number in your bond squad scorecard.

What affects the beta rating in a bond mutual fund? The most significant factor is the duration of the bonds it holds. As you have learned, the longer the duration period, the higher the chances of interest rates going up and damaging the value of the bonds.

Since we are on the subject of duration, let's check the average duration period of the bonds in this mutual fund.

Forever Is Too Long

At Morningstar.com, click the "Portfolio" heading in the left navigational bar. Your screen should look something like this:

[3] For an intermediate-term bond fund, a beta lower than .98 percent is considered stable. And for long-term bond funds, a beta lower than 1.12 percent is considered stable.

Style Box Details

Average Eff Duration	1.6 Yrs
Average Eff Maturity	2.01 Yrs
Average Credit Quality	A

Source: www.morningstar.com

Note the average effective duration of the fund you're researching on your scorecard.

The average duration for this fund is 1.6 years. This is a very short period of time in the life of a bond. Remember that by definition, the average duration of a short-term bond fund is less than 3.5 years. What this short period tells us is that the potential for volatility of this fund is low (and we have already confirmed that by also looking at this fund's beta rating). Interest rates would have to change significantly in a very short period of time to negatively affect this fund's share price.

Does Your Bond Fund Rate?

Lastly, look at the average credit rating for your fund's bonds. It is important to note the creditworthiness of the companies to whom you are lending your hard-earned money. You will find this information in the same place you found the fund's average duration period.

Take a look at the previous chart. This fund's holdings have an average credit rating of A.

Write the credit rating in the appropriate box on your bond squad scorecard.

Who Gets to Be Next?

Now that you have written down the most pertinent information about your first fund, go back to your screening list. Which fund would you choose to look up next?

Let me help you a little bit. Which fund has the highest five-year

total return record? Fund B does. How is its important three-year
record? It happens to have the second highest three-year total return.
Because the returns of those two years are so similar (at 6.68 percent
and 6.59 percent), they are thus considered stable. Remember: *The
smaller the difference between each period's returns the better.* So Fund B has
a stable total return that dates back five years and stays strong. That's
good.

Write down your next mutual fund name in your bond squad scorecard and fill in your total return figures where they correspond. Take a
look at the three- and five-year returns and remember to look for stability. The less variation in total returns over the years, the better. Now
go through the other funds to get a top four list. First, look to see who
has a five-year return. Next, look at the three-year return and compare
it to the five-year. Write down the funds according to this difference,
favoring those whose difference is smaller. Remember that stability is
important. If the difference between the three- and five-year total
returns is the same, give preference to the fund with the higher three-
year return.

My list would include the bond funds in the following order:

1. Bond Fund F (because it has a ten-year record and stable returns).

2. Bond Fund B (because it has a five-year record, a difference of .09 between the five- and three-year
   returns, and is the only fund that beats its three-year
   return but doesn't have a five-year record).

3. Bond Fund G (because it has a five-year record, a difference of .09 between the five- and three-year record,
   and the next highest three-year return within the three
   funds with this .09 difference).

4. Bond Fund I (because it has a five-year record, a difference of .09 when compared to the three-year return, and the next highest return of those funds that have a difference of .09 between their three-year and five-year returns).

Once you have identified the most stable funds with the highest returns during the past three years, it is time to begin our final inspection. You will do this by going through the process outlined above to fill in the scorecard.

I have made up the numbers in the following scorecard, and they do not represent any actual mutual funds on this or any other date. This example is for illustration purposes only for you to learn the evaluation process.

This is what my scorecard looks like now:

BOND SQUAD SCORECARD

Fund Name	Total Return					Yield	Fees				Beta	Avg. Credit Rating	Avg. Duration
	1-Yr Return	Net 1-Yr Return	3-Yr Return	5-Yr Return	10-Yr Return		Front-end	Back-end	Expense Ratio	12 (b)1			
F	9.35	9.35	6.39	6.48	6.18	4.6	0	0	.56	0	.38	A	1.6
B	9.73	7.23	6.68	6.59	-	8.02	2.5	0	.56	0	.38	AAA	1.5
G	9.40	6.90	6.36	6.27	-	6.22	2.5	0	.60	0	.48	AA	3.7
I	7.15	7.15	6.10	6.19	-	7.00	0	0	.65	0	.49	A	2.5

The Moment of Truth

Just as we did with stock funds, we have narrowed down our choices to four funds that are all competing for a place in our hearts—and our wallets. The differences among them may be subtle once we get to this point. This is why we will need our eagle eyes to spot the weak links that may backfire on us later on.

Read the prospectus for each fund and look for the type of investments that the manager uses to boost profits. Sometimes a bond fund can have stocks in its portfolio and still be considered a bond fund. This is not necessarily bad, but double-check your beta rating and best-fit index to make sure that those stocks are not making the fund more volatile than its peers. Other times, a bond fund tries to beat the competition by sprinkling its holdings with lower-rated junk bonds. This may increase the dividend rate of a fund, but it can also get you in trouble if any of those companies default on their loans.

So to further narrow our search, let's begin by disqualifying one of the funds. Look over the list. The first place to look at is the yield. Are they all paying a yield that is lower than their total return during the past year? Yes. Good. Now let's get deeper: Subtract the yield from the *one-year* total returns, and see which fund got to keep a higher profit.

Fund I paid out 7 percent in yield while its total one-year return was 7.15 percent. That left .15 percent in actual share price growth after dividends. The total return was lower than the other funds during the past three and five years, its beta is the highest on the list, and it also has the highest fees. We just found our weakest link. Adios Fund I!

Fund F, on the other hand, has the highest total return after subtracting its yield, because when you take away 4.6 percent from this fund's total return of 9.35 percent, you are still left with 4.75 percent. It has one of the lowest expense ratios on the list. Its beta rating is also among the lowest, and it has the second-lowest duration period. This fund also has a long track record since it shows a ten-year total return. This would be my number-one choice.

Fund B has a much narrower return after paying its dividends (1.71 percent), and it hasn't been around for ten years. Its beta is good, but when I take into account its expense ratio *and* its front-end load, I see that the fees are eroding this fund's bottom line. The cover charge is very high for this exclusive club. See ya, Fund B!

Fund G also has a cover charge in the form of a front-end load, and its duration period is the longest here with an average of 3.7 years. Pass on Fund G.

So, it looks like Fund F is the best-performing short-term bond fund in this case.

Adding Hybrid Funds to the Mix

As we previously mentioned, hybrid funds add an extra kick to a portfolio that is beginning to wind down, because hybrids include stocks in its holdings, and stocks have a greater potential for gains over time than bonds.

Before we go on to the method of evaluating a hybrid fund, here is a chart on the next page that will give you an idea of how this type of fund compares to bond mutual funds. By comparing the following table to the funds you just evaluated, you may find that you will gravitate toward one or the other or that you wish to incorporate the power of both types of mutual funds into your investment portfolio as you get closer to your end goal. Bond funds may add stability to a mutual fund mix, but over time, you will still need to have some stocks in your holdings to reach the highest potential earnings. If you look back at the Asset Allocation Table on page 134 that shows you how to rebalance your mutual funds as you approach your financial goal, you will see that I include domestic hybrid funds during the slowdown period. If you are investing to generate income, it is in your best interest to keep one-third of your mutual funds in domestic hybrid funds. Just like a good classic car, they keep a higher resale value.

Let's take a look at the vital signs for the domestic (meaning U.S.) hybrid mutual funds for the last fifteen years up to October 31, 2000, as reported by Morningstar, Inc. Here it is:

DOMESTIC HYBRID FUNDS

1-yr total return	7.96%
3-yr avg. total return	9.04%
5-yr avg. total return	12.20%
10-yr avg. total return	12.59%
15-yr avg. total return	11.46%
Average yield	2.65%
Average beta (when compared to S&P 500 Index)	0.52%

Source: Morningstar®Principia® Pro

As you can see, the average historical returns of these mutual funds are very respectable, and yet their average beta is very low. That spells a great opportunity for potential profit within a conservative frame. As such, I urge you to consider domestic hybrid funds, even if you consider yourself a very conservative investor. Anyone interested in learning more about them, read on.

On the Road Again: Evaluating Hybrid or Moderate Allocation Funds

Since hybrid funds have the characteristics of both stock and bond funds, you will have the opportunity to combine what you have learned so far in the process of evaluating this breed of mutual fund.

Go to www.morningstar.com and on the top navigational bar click on the "Mutual Fund Screener" link. This is the starting point for our research.

Now click on the "Morningstar Category" section and choose "Moderate Allocation." Your screen should look like this:

Set Criteria

Fund Type   ☼ Fund group: | All | ⬍ |

              ☼ Morningstar Category: | Moderate Allocation | ⬍ |

              ☼ Manager tenure greater than or equal to: | Any | ⬍ |

Source: www.morningstar.com

Now scroll down to the middle of the Morningstar screen where you can see the "Ratings and Risk" section. Remember the category rating in The Five Rs? This is the grading system used by Morningstar to rate how well a mutual fund balances itself on that tightrope between greed and fear. We deserve nothing but the best, so check off the box next to the highest possible rating under the "Morningstar® Category Rating™," the circled number five.

Now go a little lower to the "Category risk better than or equal to" section and open the drop-down window to the right of it. Find the word "Low" and choose it. Again, we don't want to gamble with our money, so we are requesting to see the most stable group of funds in the domestic hybrid category. Here is what your screen should look like now:

Ratings and Risk   Check all the ratings that you would like to include:

              ☼ Morningstar Star Rating
              ☐ ★
              ☐ ★★
              ☐ ★★★
              ☐ ★★★★
              ☐ ★★★★★
              ☐ New, unrated funds

              ☼ Morningstar Risk better than or equal to: | Below Average | ▼ |

Source: www.morningstar.com

Now go to the bottom of the screen and click on the button that says "Show Results." On the new screen that appears you will see the word "View:" with a drop-down window with the word "Snapshot." Open this drop-down window and choose "Performance." This option will show us all these funds according to their total return performance. Once you see the list, double click on the underlined "3-Year Return (%)" column heading so your trusty machine sorts the funds by this important statistic.

This is what my screen looked like when I followed these instructions. I am using imaginary names instead of the real fund names.

Fund Name	Category Risk	YTD Return (%)	1–Year Return (%)	▼ 3–Year Return (%)	5–Year Return (%)	10–Year Return (%)
Hybrid Fund A	Low	1.47	19.18	13.54	14.48	--
Hybrid Fund B	Low	7.60	27.87	11.92	13.88	12.94
Hybrid Fund C	Low	6.05	12.56	11.12	11.66	9.46
Hybrid Fund D	Low	1.16	8.46	9.38	9.64	--

Source: www.morningstar.com

If your list shows more than four funds, limit yourself to the first four, using the same criteria we used to identify the best four bond funds: longevity of track record rates first, difference in total return for the three- and five-year period next, and three-year total return last.

Now repeat our mantra: *track record and stability*. Look for the fund that has the longest track record and the most stability in their total returns. Remember that we are looking at the best of the group, so these members of this elite club will all have their individual merits. It may feel like splitting hairs at this point, but this exercise is well worth it, since you may find one particular piece of information that will sway your investment decision.

You will need both scorecards, the one we used for stocks, the fund candidates scorecard (on page 119 in chapter 8), and our bond squad scorecard (on page 160 in this chapter), since we are dealing with a mutual fund that has both types of investments. Make a clean copy of each scorecard or print them out from www.JulieStav.com. Now fill in the scorecards for your top four choices. If you forget any steps, simply go back and reread how to get the numbers.

Use your fund candidates scorecard first, and then click on the "Top 25 Holdings" section of the Morningstar.com report to find out the bond characteristics of that particular fund. In some cases, you may find that a credit rating and average duration are not provided. What you then should do is click on "Bond Quality" under the "Portfolio" heading on the left navigational bar. Here you will see the credit rating of the bonds this fund is holding. We will settle for nothing less than A. You should be wary if the fund holds bonds rated less than BBB. If under "Bond Quality" you see "U.S. Gov't," you should consider these even higher than AAA.

If, for some reason, there is nothing listed under bond quality, you should check the fund's prospectus. Go to www.sec.gov/edgar/searchedgar/prospectus.htm, type in the fund, and click on the most recent report available. (To review how to find a prospectus see page 57.) There are two areas that you should focus on when evaluating a hybrid fund:

1. *Principal risks of investing in the portfolio.* Be on the look-out for anything that indicates that the fund takes additional risks by investing in junk bonds or bonds rated below investment grade. We want to make sure this fund isn't engaging in any practices that increase the chances of losing money.

2. *How the portfolio invests.* This section will tell you if the fund invests in low-grade bonds.

If after careful reading you still can't tell what types of bonds the fund holds, call the toll-free number on the prospectus. Ask for the credit ratings of the fund's bond holdings. Don't be afraid to ask for the information. Be an educated investor so you can make the smartest financial choices.

After you fill out your scorecards, read the prospectus for each fund. Check out the top holdings of each company and see if among them you can identify any company toward which you may have a strong feeling, either positive or negative. Read the section regarding risk and the one that addresses the strategy that the managers will use to try to increase profits. It will tell you there if the fund should be considered riskier than others in its category. You don't have to sell your soul to make money in mutual funds. Once you have identified the leaders in their field as you have up to now, you can allow yourself the privilege of a subjective decision.

As in any bond fund, look for any signs of boosters that the managers of the mutual fund may use to increase its returns. This will be spelled out in the prospectus.

You may wish to read the analysts' comments on the "Data Interpreter" section of your mutual fund report at www.morningstar.com. But remember that you are reading someone's opinion rather than actual facts. The prospectus, on the other hand, has to pass scrutiny of the SEC before it ever gets to you, the investor, and the information in it must be factual.

Once you have done all your research, it's time to decide which fund is best for you. Do as we did when we chose bond funds. Here is the process to refresh your memory:

1. Find the fund(s) with the longest track record.

2. Look at their three-year total return.

3. Subtract the three-year from the five-year return. Write down the difference.

4. Now, start with the smallest difference and look at the three-year return. Is it competitive when you look at

the rest of the funds on your list? If it rates first or second, write that fund down.

5. Continue on your list, following this process until you have covered all your candidates.

To Make a Long Story Short

Throughout this book, you have now learned how to evaluate many different kinds of mutual funds, whether growth or income, stock- or bond-based. The main factors to consider in evaluating any mutual fund are:

1. *Total returns.* Since track record is important, the longer the fund has been in existence, the better. But besides longevity, *we want stability.* Remember that the three-year return is one of our most significant gauges, but check out how stable the fund is by comparing three-, five-, and if available, ten-year returns.

2. *Fees.* Make sure that you look at any front- or back-end fees and then subtract them from the one-year total return to get an accurate look at what your net profits will be for that time period.

3. *Risk.* Growth funds have more risk than income funds. Remember to measure the fund's risk against its best-fit index's volatility.

4. *Yield.* Make sure that you check your mutual fund's yield. It must be lower than your one-year return. If it isn't, disqualify that fund immediately!

Now that you have learned how to choose among mutual funds'
more conservative choices as you near your goal, in the next chapter I
will show you how to reallocate or rebalance your investments to bring
them in line with your need to generate income.

CHAPTER ELEVEN

Fine-Tuning Your Investment Strategy to Get the Right Mix

After all those years of investing wisely and contributing to your fund, the prospect of collecting your well-deserved pot of money is exciting.

Congratulate yourself; you deserve it! You set financial goals, researched investment options, and diligently and consistently invested money into your funds of choice. Then you sat back—checking on your investments periodically to make sure you were staying on the right track—and watched your money grow at an outstanding rate due to the power of mutual fund investing.

Now, as you get closer to your goal, closer to the time when you're going to start using that money, you need to shift gears.

This doesn't mean your money is no longer going to grow like it once did, but now your primary concern is preserving what you have already accumulated.

As you discovered in chapter 10, when you get two to five years from your long-term goal, you move into a transition phase. If you are a long-term investor with a growth objective working toward a nest egg that can generate monthly income for your retirement years, you transition to an investor with a mixed objective (growth and income). You need the income funds to generate immediate money to live off of, but you still want growth funds that will continue to increase the size of your nest egg so you don't have to worry about it drying up.

You'd use the same investment strategy if you came into a lump sum that you want to live off of right now. You want to allocate some money into an income fund so that you can generate a monthly nut to pay for your dreams, but you don't want that money to run out, so some money stays in a growth fund.

Even if you've been investing in order to amass a sum of money that you will withdraw all at once—say for a college fund or house down payment—you still have to adjust your investments as you near your goal. As we discussed throughout this book, it is the nature of mutual funds that they can experience temporary low points. It would be tragic if, when the time comes for you to withdraw your hard-earned booty, the fund has taken a downturn and you lose money. For this reason, I recommend that when you are five years away from your goal, you begin to move your money into more stable, conservative accounts, such as bond and hybrid funds. You might not get as high a return, but there is a greater chance that your fund will maintain its value.

In investment lingo, this rebalancing of funds is referred to as *reallocating*.

In the previous chapter, you learned how to evaluate and choose the best bond funds and hybrid funds. Now you will find out how much of your investment should be in those bond and hybrid funds and whether or not to leave some in stock-based mutual funds. You will see how to reallocate your accounts as you approach D-day (*D* is for *distribution*).

Learning to adjust your mutual fund accounts to accommodate your current lifestyle will give you the freedom to use your hard-earned money without guilt and will assure you that it lasts for as long as you need it.

How to Stuff Your Investment Drawers

On this page is an Asset Allocation Table, which you got a peek at earlier, to help you adjust your mutual funds as you get closer to D-day. As you can see, it is divided into two parts. The left side of the table deals with investments in which the goal is to accumulate and withdraw one lump

ASSET ALLOCATION TABLE

Years away from goal date	Lump Sum Distribution from Your Investments				Income-Generating Investments			
	Portion of your total investment in each investment category				Portion of your total investment in each investment category			
	Stock Mutual Funds	Domestic Hybrid Funds	Bond Funds	Money Market Mutual Funds	Stock Mutual Funds	Domestic Hybrid Funds	Bond Funds	Money Market Mutual Funds
5	1/2	1/2	-0-	-0-	1/2	1/2	-0-	-0-
4	1/3	1/3	1/3	-0-	1/3	1/3	1/3	-0-
3*	-0-	1/3	2/3	Dividends and capital gains	1/3	1/3	1/3	Dividends and capital gains
2	-0-			T-bills and/or money market mutual funds	1/3	1/3	1/3	Any amount you wish to have readily accessible to you within two years**

* Open a money market mutual find account and begin receiving capital gains and dividend distributions in cash as a direct deposit into this account.

** Every year transfer monies from your mutual funds into your money market fund as needed. Always transfer money from the accounts that are showing the highest returns at the time into your money market fund.

sum of money. The right-side section applies to income-generating investments, such as retirement funds.

The purpose of rearranging your investments is to preserve the gains you have managed to accumulate but also keep your earning power at full throttle for as long as possible.

As long as your goal is five years away or longer, keep your money fully invested in stock mutual funds. But as you approach your desired financial destination, begin to redistribute your investments so you end up with the right mix of stocks and bonds.

How to Work It: Income-Generating Investments

So what does this all mean? Let's just say that when you were in your thirties you decided to start stashing money away so you could stop working for a living at sixty. You had plenty of time to reach the goal, so you chose one or two mutual funds in the most profitable category, which is growth funds. These are the mutual funds that buy stocks with your money. Assume that you are now fifty-five, five years away from your retirement age of sixty, when you wish to stop working and begin withdrawing money from your nest egg to pay for your daily expenses and dreams.

Well, according to our Asset Allocation Table, when you are five years away from your goal, you should begin evaluating domestic hybrid funds, and choose the best one. Keep half of the money you have in the stock fund and transfer the other half into the hybrid fund so that you end up with equal amounts in each type of investment. You can do this by dividing your stock fund amount in half and then selling all of it at once, or you can do it in smaller amounts, say over a six-month period. Your tax accountant may have some input here, since you will have some tax consequences if these funds are not inside an official IRA or 401(k) retirement account, so make sure you consult with him/her.

Now you have two types of accounts: a growth account in a stock fund and a domestic hybrid account, which holds stocks and bonds.

Four years before your retirement, you are going to make another adjustment. Research the best bond fund you can find. Then add up the account (balances of your stock and hybrid funds) and divide that amount by three. For example, if you had $210,000 total when you added the two accounts, when you divided the total by three, you will get $70,000. Leave $70,000 in the stock fund and $70,000 in the hybrid fund. Use the money that you withdrew from these funds (which should also be $70,000) to open a bond fund account. The end result will be that you will have one-third of your money in a stock fund, one-third in domestic hybrid, and one-third in a bond fund.

Three years from retirement, you will open a money market mutual fund, if you don't already have one, and request from your existing mutual funds that they send all dividends and capital gains to your money market account. This will begin to siphon your investments into the holding tank (your money market account) that you will use as the direct source of income.

Two years before retirement, take a look at your mutual fund accounts and take some money from the one or two that are giving you the highest returns and transfer it to your money market account. Deposit whatever amount you wish to have readily available to you within two years. Maybe you transfer two years' worth of bills, or perhaps that's too much and you would rather have just one year's worth at a time. The goal here is to leave in your three types of mutual funds (stock, hybrid, and bond funds) whatever you are willing to do without for two years or longer and deposit what you want accessible within two years into your money market fund.

One year away from retirement, you would only do your normal checkup on your funds, continue to have your dividends and capital gains deposited into your money market account, and get ready to enjoy your new lifestyle. Yeehaw!

Each year after that, as you review your investments, transfer money from the mutual funds that are doing the best at the time into your money market mutual fund to replenish your spending pot. Doable? I see it all the time.

How to Work It:
Lump-Sum Distribution Investments

Maybe you're not investing for income. Maybe your goal is to make a major purchase or cover a mega expense (such as the case of Tony and Amanda, who are saving for their twin girls' college education or, yikes, a double wedding). Your goal is to have enough money so you can cash out all at once or over a short period of a few years.

For this type of investor, the left-hand side of the table offers a guideline. The process is similar to the previous example, but when you are three years from your desired goal, you will take all the money from your stock funds and have your investments one-third in hybrid and two-thirds in bond funds.

Two years prior to the day when you need to cash out, you will transfer your money into a money market mutual fund account so it's ready for you when you need it. It's a pretty risky proposition to keep any money you will need within two years in the market. You don't know what the investment atmosphere will be by then, and you don't want to have to withdraw it when the mutual funds are going through one of their downturns. Better safe than sorry.

Summing It All Up

Your years of hard work and your unwavering discipline have allowed you to accumulate the funds you need to afford not to work for a living, to afford to send your children to the college of their choice, or to accomplish a desired dream.

Working your money smart means you have made sure, as you approach that celebrated moment of reaching your goal, to reallocate your investment funds away from volatility and toward more conservative stability.

You don't need to try to impress your friends and relatives with fancy investment words or spend countless hours in front of a computer every day of your life to generate respectable returns in mutual funds. All you need to do is apply the few sound principles of investing reflected in this system and let your personal financial chauffeur get you to your desired destination.

But regardless of the merits of your chosen vehicle, it pays to look out the window on your journey to financial freedom to make sure you are still going the right way. That's why you learned about spring cleaning in chapter 9 and reallocation of funds as you approached your goal.

Once you set your wheels in motion, you can go ahead and enjoy life to its fullest.

"But wait! I'm not home free yet!" you cry. "What about my retirement accounts such as my 401(k) at work? I still don't know what to do with those!" Don't unfasten your seat belts yet, because in the next chapter you will discover how to maximize the investment choices within those retirement accounts as well.

CHAPTER TWELVE

The Sleeping Giant

Danny couldn't believe it! It had been almost a year since his grandmother had given him Porky, his beloved piggy bank. Every single week he had faithfully saved most of his allowance by methodically slipping his loose change through the small crevice along Porky's spine. He was hoping to have enough money to buy a brand-new mountain bike. But as hard as he tried to keep track of his prized savings bank's contents along the way, Danny had lost count of how much money he had accumulated.

He swallowed hard as he headed for the garage with his most cherished possession in hand. Soon he would find out if his sacrifice had paid off. Danny tightened the grip on the hammer in his hand, aimed at the piggy bank, closed his eyes, and . . . Kaplooey!

Retirement accounts—those specific accounts that are exempt from taxes until you withdraw your funds at fifty-nine and a half years of age or later—offer you a tremendous opportunity to build a nest egg toward your golden years. But like Danny, many retirement account participants may wonder if the money they are accumulating over the years will be enough to fund their future dreams or to satisfy their financial needs.

If you are taking advantage of a retirement plan, whether offered through your work or acquired on your own, you have taken the first step toward arriving at the moment when you can choose to stop working for a living.

But rather than waiting until you get closer to the day you need to access your money and have to take a hammer to your bank, you can assure yourself that you will hit the mark when the time comes if you actively manage your retirement accounts along the way using the same strategies you learned for managing your other investment accounts. You may even find that you can stop working sooner than you thought or enjoy a higher monthly income during your retirement. I have seen this happen more than once.

Whatever your financial plan, regardless of your age and other financial goals, you should have at least one retirement account. No one should leave their financial life up in the air when they have the chance to fund their future. The sooner you start, the smaller the amount you will need to invest and the bigger the pot at the end of your rainbow.

Many employers offer their employees the ability to shelter money on a regular basis and invest it toward retirement. What this means is that an employee can choose to have a set amount of money taken out of her paycheck each month and put into a pension program, and this money comes out of each paycheck *before* taxes. This contribution bypasses the tax collector. In other words, instead of your having to wait to get your paycheck with its usual diminished amount due to taxes withheld and then put a portion of it into an account of your own, your employer transfers it directly into your account so you never see it—or spend it!

Being able to invest on a tax-deferred basis (which means that your account is exempt from taxes until you withdraw the money from it) is one of the smartest things you can do. This is how it works:

Let's assume that you get paid a bonus of $200. Great, huh? But when you get your bonus check, you don't see $200. Hey, hold on! What happened to your money? Is your employer cheating you? They said $200! Yes, they did, but Uncle Sam requires that your employer withhold some tax money from your $200 to pay the income taxes on that amount. Assuming that you have the correct number of withholdings from your paycheck and that you are in the 28 percent tax bracket, you will have 28 percent of your $200 withheld by your employer and sent to the federal government on your behalf. In this example we're assuming you live in a state that doesn't impose taxes in addition to federal tax. Otherwise you would have to pay state tax on this money as well. And some companies even end up taxing bonuses so much that you only get half! To make it simpler here, we're going to assume the 28 percent tax that results in $56 deducted from the original $200. You don't lose that $56. It's applied toward your tax bill at the end of the year, but right now you get a check for the difference, which is $200 minus $56, or $144.

You're not going to blow that money on that cute pair of shoes you saw downtown (although it is tempting). No, smart, responsible you is going to invest that money. You invest your $144 and you earn 10 percent on it a year (just to make our math more palatable). At the end of the first year, you will have: $144 plus 10 percent or $158.40

Oh, but we're not done with you yet! Uncle Sam is going to want 28 percent of the *interest* you are earning each year as well! You earned $14.40 the first year (10 percent of $144), so you have to pay another $2.88 in taxes, leaving you now a net balance at the end of the first year of $155.52 ($158 minus $2.88 that went to taxes). So your $200 bonus ended up at $155.52, even after you invested it for one year at 10 percent! Drat!

But what if you take this $200, invest it in a tax-deferred retirement fund, bypass the tax man, and *then* earn your 10 percent? By the end of your first investment year, you would have had $200 plus 10 percent or $220.

Since your account is sheltered from taxes because it is in a retirement account, that means that Uncle Sam doesn't get to tap into your profits yet, so you don't have to share your 10 percent gain with him. Your $200 bonus turned into $220 if you invested it tax-deferred—much better than the $152.52 you ended up with outside your retirement program.

This is just $200, and this is only over a one-year period. I won't bore you with the details, but trust me when I tell you that since you are now earning interest on top of interest (remember our buddy-pal-buddy Mr. Compound Interest?), your tax-deferred retirement account begins to inflate faster than you know. The difference in account balances between investing outside and inside your retirement program gets even wider as time goes by.

I can just hear you say, "Sure, Julie, but when I withdraw the money, I'll have to pay more in taxes!" Yes, you are right, you will pay taxes based on the larger balance, *but you will get to keep more money, too*. And isn't that what this book is all about? Since you have used some of the money you would have had to pay in taxes to invest, your account balance is much greater in the end, and even though you will pay taxes on that amount, you will end up with a higher balance than you would have had if you had paid the taxes on your profits along the way.

You may already have one or more of the following types of retirement accounts. If you do, make a firm commitment to work them hard to boost your investment power by applying the principles you have learned in this book and choosing the best available investments among your given options.

Gee, now that you see the benefits, wanna know how you can get to invest tax-deferred? Here are a few of the choices available to you.

IRAs

Short for Individual Retirement Account, an IRA now comes in three flavors:

- *Tax Deductible IRAs.* These IRA plans allow you to invest on a tax-deferred basis, meaning that you don't pay taxes on your account until you actually take the money out. Each year, you may put aside the amount allowed by the IRS and invest it toward your retirement without having to pay taxes on your initial investment or the gains you accumulate along the way, just like our $200 bonus example above. There are certain restrictions that are worth checking into before opening an

IRA account. I will give you more information on where to get this information at the end of this section.

- *Education IRA.* A new twist on another type of "retirement account," this type of IRA gives you the opportunity to invest and keep the gains away from taxes altogether. *This account accrues profits tax free, not just tax deferred!* Uncle Sam doesn't get to tap on these accounts at all! An education IRA allows you to put aside a yearly contribution of up to $500 per child as long as he/she is under eighteen years of age.

  The purpose of an education IRA is to accumulate money to pay for tuition, books, supplies, fees, or other expenses associated with higher education for that child, even if a student is only attending on a part-time basis.

  The main advantage to this type of IRA is that when you withdraw the money, both the earnings as well as the contribution amounts will be tax free. The reason you don't pay taxes on the amount you deposited over the years is that you do *not* get to deduct it from your taxable income when you invested the money. The fact that you don't pay any taxes on the gains is a gift! Over the years, this tax break compounds and results in a tremendous boost for any investment account.

- *Roth IRA.* If you open this type of retirement account and hold it for at least five years, you will, at age fifty-nine and a half, have access to the money you have accumulated in it over the years without having to pay one penny in taxes. You may also bypass taxes if you use the money to buy your first home or if you become disabled. If you need to withdraw money from a Roth IRA for any other purpose, you only have to pay taxes on the gains in your account, not on your original deposit, since the deposits that go into a Roth IRA have to see Uncle Sam before they go into the account at the time you invested it.

In an IRA, whether a traditional IRA, a Roth, or an Education IRA, you have the freedom to invest in almost anything you want. The only investments you are not allowed to make are in collectibles or precious metals, with the exception of U.S. gold and silver bullion. Otherwise, the sky's the limit in your investment smorgasbord choices.

You can go to www.irs.ustreas.gov/forms_pubs to read Publication 590, a complete guide to IRA accounts and their latest restrictions. You may also order this publication directly from the Internal Revenue Service by calling (800) 829-3676.

How to Evaluate IRAs

The selection process for choosing the best mutual fund for your IRA account is based on:

1. *Time before retirement age.* If you are at least five years away from fifty-nine and a half, you are still a growth investor; choose growth options available to you in mutual funds. If you are between two and five years from retirement, you are a transitional investor, which includes both growth and income mutual fund choices; look at the Asset Allocation Table on page 134 to figure out how to allocate your funds. And if you are two years or less from retirement and planning to supplement your monthly retirement income from your IRA account, you would distribute your investments within your IRAs very conservatively, also using the Asset Allocation Table.

2. *Merits of each individual investment option.* Use the same steps you have learned in this book to guide you through the process of choosing the best IRA investment for you. Whether you are in the growth stage, the transition stage, or the distribution stage, you now know how to choose the best mutual fund in each of these categories to maximize your profits. Use your newly found knowledge and put it to work right away, even if you already have an IRA that is sitting somewhere collecting dust. Shake it off and make it produce for you mercilessly!

401(k) and 403(b)

These plans are quirky but ultracool. If you have one available to you, especially one with a matching program, *take advantage of it.* Have no idea what I am talking about? Keep reading.

Many employers offer 401(k) pension plans to their employees. In a 401(k) plan, a certain percentage of your salary is deducted from your paycheck, bypassing Uncle Sam altogether, and going directly into your account. In addition to protecting you from taxes, under a 401(k) your employer will often match part of your contributions. Imagine that! That means that if you deposit $100 in your 401(k) account, and your employer deposits another $100 in your account on your behalf, you have just made a 100 percent profit without even trying! Can you say, "free money"? *Don't pass up this bargain!*

But there is a catch with 401(k) plans. Your investment choices are limited to those that are offered by your employer, and your investment must be automatically deducted from your salary through payroll deduction. You cannot physically write a check to deposit into your employer-sponsored 401(k) account.

The 403(b) plans are pretty similar to 401(k) plans. If you work for a nonprofit organization, such as a museum, public school, zoo (no, if your workplace *feels* like a zoo, it does not count), or a charity, you may have this type of retirement account available to you. A 403(b) plan acts pretty much like its cousin the 401(k), since it allows you to put aside a monthly amount that goes directly to your investment account through payroll deduction.

Employers do not usually match in 403(b) plans. The best way to maximize this retirement plan is to request a list of all your investment choices from your payroll office. Most likely you will have a choice of annuities (which are savings accounts within insurance companies) and mutual funds. You cannot invest in individual stocks within a 403(b) program since it is not allowed by law.

Follow the same process as the one I cover for choosing a mutual fund inside an IRA program, by first determining if you are a growth, transition, or income investor. Then, evaluate the investment options available to you. You are also limited in your choices. Choose one among those that fall within your investment objective. Use the principles we have covered in this book to identify the available mutual funds that have the biggest gain potential.

Don't let the fact that your investment is under a pension umbrella either scare you away or lull you into a feeling of safety. The process of choosing the best mutual fund for you, whether it's inside or outside your pension program, is the same. And it's up to you to make the right choices. If you are opening an IRA account, first choose your investment using our system. Then request an IRA application (they have different ones for each type of IRA). That's all there is to it.

Your 401(k) and 403(b) accounts are opened through your employer, and they will provide you with the necessary forms to do it. However, they will not help you choose an investment. In most cases, a coworker will try to help you by telling you what they are investing in, and we both know that their objective might be different from yours or they may be close to retirement while you may be barely out of your teens. So how do you choose? Learn to take charge of your own destiny by making the decisions that apply to you and only you. It may not make very good party conversation over a glass of bubbly, but it's the surest way to financial freedom.

Waking Up the Sleeping Giant

Make a concerted effort to take charge of your employer-sponsored retirement account and feel the power of this sleeping giant. By putting aside as much as possible in your 401(k), you are taking on Uncle Sam as your partner, since you will see your account grow not only by the deposits that you and your employer may make, but also by being able to invest and accumulate compound interest on monies that would have otherwise gone to pay for income taxes.

Find out how much money you are allowed to put aside toward your retirement, and give until it hurts! If the maximum contribution is, for example, 6 percent of your gross income before taxes, give every cent of that if you can, especially if your employer has a matching program. Your money can grow faster in a 401(k) than in most other retirement accounts just on the basis of what the employer matches, regardless of the profits over the long term! If you cannot contribute the maximum, don't be afraid to start smaller. Whatever you can invest will all add up in the end.

There are a few questions you need to know the answers to before you can make better decisions with your 401(k). So before you sign on the dotted line, ask your human resources representative the following four questions:

1. Does your employer match your contributions and to what extent?

2. When are you vested in your retirement account— meaning that you own the whole enchilada, and you could take it with you even if you were to change jobs?

3. Ask for the investment menu that is at your disposal when choosing among potential investments for your 401(k) account. This simply refers to the choices of investments that they are allowing you. Don't just

accept the category (stocks, bonds, money market, etc.), get the names of the stocks and funds if available.

4. Find out how often you can make changes in your 401(k) choices and what the procedure is for doing so, should you wish to readjust your investment decisions at any point. Most companies have a thirty-day period at the beginning or end of every fiscal year when they allow you to rebalance your account if you so choose. Find out the details, and write it into your calendar so you don't forget. Then, a month before that date, also write in a reminder to yourself that that date is approaching, so you can do some research and figure out if you are still on track.

Armed with the list of possible candidates, your first step is to determine how far away you are from fifty-nine and a half years of age, since that is the magic age when you can begin to withdraw your retirement funds without having to deal with government penalties. Remember that you are making a commitment to do without this account until retirement age. Don't invest any money into your 401(k) that you have allocated to any other purpose.

Once you determine how long you have until retirement, you are ready to choose your personal investment allocation. "Yak! Cough, cough, cough! What in the world is *that*?" you ask. Asset allocation is nothing more than the process of making a decision of whether to concentrate your investments among stocks, bonds, domestic hybrid funds, money market accounts, CDs—whatever choices are available in your employer's investment menu.

As we have seen in chapter 10, your proximity to retirement will determine your appropriate investment categories. Again, if you are five or more years away from retirement, you should concentrate on funds with a growth objective. That is, funds that have more risk but more payoff. If you are two to five years away, you need to transition from growth objective funds to a mixture of growth objective and income-generating objective funds. Two years or less to retirement? If your retirement account is to provide you with income, keep a mix of growth, hybrid, and bonds in your mutual funds (using the Asset Allocation Table on page 134). If you want to cash in all at once, it's time to park your money in a safe, shady spot so it's available when you need it. Because you need your money in two years or less, you don't want to tie it up in any type of fund. Saving accounts, CDs, T-bills, and money market accounts are the way to go. See chapter 4 for details. The only difference in how you allocate your money in an employer-sponsored retirement fund compared to how you do so in any other fund is that in 401(k) and 403(b) accounts your choices are limited to those offered by your employer. Most participants in employer-related retirement programs base their investment choices on the well-meaning recommendations of someone close to them that they trust: the human resources person who is handing you the papers to fill out and sign or a colleague at work. Remember: That well-meaning person may be sending you on an erroneous path by projecting his or her own personal needs and solutions onto yours. What may apply to them does not necessarily fit your individual circumstances, risk tolerance, time horizon, or subjective inclinations.

You don't have to wait until it's time to take the hammer to your retirement piggy bank to make sure you are investing in the smartest, most profitable way possible. Learning to manage your retirement plans is akin to periodically taking an X-ray picture of your piggy bank's contents. By monitoring its progress, you will be able to focus your investments in a way that will generate the best profits and reflect your own distinctive personality. Nobody does it like you do.

Here is a simple guide that will help you understand and handle what may seem like the overwhelming task of choosing among retirement investments.

Making Choices from the Employer's Investment Menu

Remember how we narrowed down our potential mutual funds from thousands of possible choices to a manageable number? When you choose among the investments offered to you by your employer, chances are the original number will be much smaller than our previous starting point. Why? Because your employer will already have made some choices on your behalf. Still confused? Don't worry, I'll get you going!

Employers usually offer a mixture of annuities (which are investments held by insurance companies), stocks (mostly their own), and mutual funds (our investment of choice). Unless you are well-versed in the field of choosing individual winning stocks, you are better off choosing mutual fund investments. Another reason to choose mutual funds in your work-related retirement account is that if you choose individual stocks, you must sit on them until the next open period in which the company allows changes in your account, so you cannot baby-sit your individual stocks and react appropriately should the market experience a major change. With a mutual fund the money manager can baby-sit each individual stock in a growth account for you.

Many employers restrict their investment choices to those that are within a particular family of funds. For example, Oppenheimer may have a pension package that assists employers in designing and implementing their employee retirement programs. In exchange, that employer only offers the mutual funds that form the Oppenheimer family. Whatever the restrictions, your goal is to use all the information available to you to identify the best investment candidate for you.

Let's pretend that your employer offers the following mutual funds. Your initial list might look like this, with the names of the funds in the family as well as their corresponding ticker symbols:

Fund A (AAAA)

Fund B (BBBB)

Fund C (CCCC)

Fund D (DDDD)

Fund E (EEEE)

Fund F (FFFF)

Fund G (GGGG)

Go to www.morningstar.com and click on the "Mutual Fund Compare" link.

Once you are on that page, in the "Enter tickers" box, enter each one of the fund symbols of the mutual funds you were given by your employer. Type a comma between each symbol. If you don't know the symbols, click on the "Ticker lookup" link right next to the "Enter tickers" heading above the box to find them.

Here, I have entered the ticker symbols from my example above. Your screen should look something like this:

Select Funds

(1) Enter fund symbols. Then, click Add to list. You may also use the Fund Comparison Ideas pop-up menu.

Enter tickers Ticker lookup

> AAAA, BBBB, CCCC, DDDD, EEEE, FFFF, GGGG

Separate fund tickers with commas.

Fund Comparison Ideas

(2) Review your list, then click Show Comparison to view your results.

To remove a fund or comparison list, click on its name and then click Remove.

Source: www.morningstar.com

Next, click on the light aqua blue button labeled "Add to List." You will see the symbols appear in a small box directly underneath it.

Now click on the "Show Comparison" button at the bottom of your screen. And here they come! All the mutual funds are lined up like little soldiers on your screen! Print this screen.

Here is what mine looked like:

Fund Name	Morningstar Analysis	Message Board	Morningstar Category	Morningstar Star Rating	YTD Return (%)	Expense Ratio (%)
Fund A	01-11-01	⌀	Large Growth	★★★★★	-9.09	0.62
Fund B	03-08-01	⌀	Europe	★★★★	-8.46	1.05
Fund C	10-17-00	⌀	Interm Term Gov	★★★★	2.39	0.63
Fund D	03-05-01	⌀	Large Growth	★★★★	-18.90	0.85
Fund E	01-29-01	⌀	Large Blend	★★★★	-4.35	0.74
Fund F	01-08-01	⌀	Large Growth	★★	-17.61	0.74
Fund G	12-06-00	⌀	Domestic Hybrid	★★★★	0.69	0.64

Source: www.morningstar.com

If you can, print out your results screen. When you have finished analyzing off-line which ones to eliminate, you can go back to your screen on-line and actually do so. Let's keep going.

Establishing a Pecking Order

Now that you have a way to explore the details of the employer-offered funds in our example, follow these steps to guide you through the elimination process:

STEP 1. *Disqualify any specialized funds*, which are those that invest all their money in a particular industry or any *foreign funds*, those mutual funds that invest all their money exclusively outside the United States. The reason for this initial screening is that both *specialized* and *foreign* mutual funds require closer scrutiny because of their volatility. By investing in only one industry or in an emerging market outside the United States, a mutual fund increases its vulnerability to sudden changes, be they political or economical, that will have a direct impact on its investment returns. You will do better in the long run by investing in mutual funds that diversify their holdings among many industries. The primary reason for holding a mutual fund rather than owning individual stock in a single company is the fact that mutual funds offer diversification by spreading their money among many different companies. Don't put all your eggs in one basket by limiting your choice to an emerging country or a popular sector. *For your retirement choices, choose among U.S. companies and diversified funds.* In this example, therefore, we would click the "Remove" button for Fund B, since it is a specialized fund that invests primarily in Europe. Adios Fund B!

STEP 2. *Concentrate on your objective.* If you are investing for *growth*, eliminate any mutual fund whose objective is *income*. In this example, we'll assume that you are seven years away from retirement and are more concerned with building your nest egg. Thus, we are focusing on growth and can exclude any bond funds. Fund C is an intermediate-term government *bond* fund. You would consider this fund if you were nearing your retirement age, but since we are assuming that you have a long time before you're ready for retirement, we'll remove that fund from our list.

STEP 3. *Check out the indexes.* This step will help us concentrate on the capitalization size and investment style that has been most profitable among growth-oriented mutual funds. Have small, medium, or large companies been leading the market in recent years, and what is the investment style that has been offering the highest rewards? Go to www.indexfunds.com to find the answer to these questions.

Open the drop-down menu next to "Data Central" and choose "Indexes." Click on the "Go" button. Put a check in the boxes for "Large Cap," "Mid Cap," and "Small Cap," as well as the small boxes next to the "Growth" and "Value" options. We are asking the computer to show us which size capitalization (large, mid, or small) and what style of company (value or growth) is at the lead in recent years.

Your screen should look like this so far:

INDEX SCREENER

Categories:	All Indexes	Total Market	Exch Composites
√ Large Cap	√ Mid Cap	√ Small Cap	Sector
√ Growth	√ Value	Bonds	Fixed Income
Global	Regional	Country	Broad Economic

Then in the "Sort by" drop-down window above all the choice boxes, choose to sort by "3-year returns." Now click on the button labeled "Screen" at the bottom of your page. You will see a list of indexes sorted by their three-year returns. It will look something like this. (Remember, your list may be different.)

	Category	3 Yr	1 Mo	3 Mo	YTD	1 Yr	5 Yr	10 Yr
Barra Mid Cap Growth	Growth	11.39	−10.83	−18.15	−18.15	−24.91	17.40	15.33
Standard & Poor's Mid Cap 400	Mid Cap	8.88	−7.43	−10.77	−10.77	−6.95	16.30	16.06
Barra Mid Cap Value	Value	6.37	−4.40	−3.44	−3.44	16.15	15.18	~
Barra Mid Cap Value	Value	6.37	−4.40	−3.44	−3.44	16.15	15.18	~

Source: www.indexfunds.com

Print out this page before going on. Now look out for the words *small*, *mid*, or *large cap* as well as the words *growth*, *value*, or *blend*. What do you find on this chart?

Well, according to the list of comparative indexes, we can see that mid caps are definitely in the lead, since they show up in the first four places. Sometimes, however, our menu of funds from our employer may *not* include a mid-cap choice. Boo! *But this can happen. We may not have access to our number-one choice of investment when making a 401(k) investment decision because our employer may not offer it.*

Before you turn off your computer and decide to give your company a piece of your mind for not offering a viable choice from among the most profitable mutual fund categories in recent years, take a look at the choices you have been given. You have come a long way from eenie mee-nie mynie moe–ing among your retirement choices, and your goal is to choose the *best* investment among your available options. The trick here is to choose wisely.

The choices of funds we do have left after we eliminated the unattractive ones in our employer example are: large growth, large blend, and domestic hybrid.

Let's see now, domestic hybrid is disqualified, since in this example we are not yet approaching retirement time, so we are not ready to start slowing down our growth potential by adding bonds to our portfolio. Bye-bye domestic hybrid. Remove Fund G from your list by putting a check in the box next to Fund G and clicking the "remove" link. The choices we have left are now between large growth and large blend.

Going back to our list of indexes, notice that the words *growth* and *value* have equal billing among the first five indexes. The term *blend* means a style of investing that combines both growth and value investing, so let's take a closer look at both choices: large growth and large blend from our 401(k) menu. You have just narrowed down your choices to four: Funds A, D, E, and F.

Now go back three clicks on your browser to bring you back to the Morningstar.com page on which we saw our list of employer-offered funds.[1] On your screen, open the box next to "Snapshot View" and select the "Performance View." Then click the underlined heading of "3-Year Return (%);" this will sort the mutual funds from the highest to the lowest returns during that period of time.

Here's what appeared on my screen.

Fund Name	YTD Return (%)	YTD (%) Rank	1-Month Return (%)	1-Month % Rank	1-Year Return (%)	1-Year % Rank	▼3-Year Return (%)	3-Year % Rank	5-Year Return (%)	5-Year % Rank
Fund A	-18.90	84	10.33	35	-27.34	55	16.93	7	17.23	14
Fund D	-4.35	24	9.20	21	-14.00	55	8.69	15	14.60	41
Fund E	-9.09	31	4.71	92	-13.92	14	8.18	41	13.84	46
Fund F	-17.61	79	14.53	6	-38.74	90	7.84	43	12.61	58

Source: www.morningstar.com

Take out a clean copy of your fund candidates scorecard and write down the name of the four funds that appear on your screen. Write down the total returns for the one-year, three-year, and five-year periods for each fund.

---

[1] If you cannot go back three clicks in your browser, simply reinput the steps as follows: 1. Go to www.morningstar.com. 2. Enter the fund's ticker symbols again in the "Enter Tickers" box of the fund, using a comma to separate each symbol. 3. Click "Add to List." 4. Click on "Show Comparison." You will now be back to where you need to be to continue our exercise.

Click on the first fund on your screen. You will see the Morningstar Quicktake® Report for that particular mutual fund.

From this point on, follow the same steps we covered in chapter 8 to rate a mutual fund. Check the Morningstar® Rating™, the beta, the fees, and the net total return. Put it all into your scorecard. Remember also to check your fund's prospectus before making the final decision. Then choose your winner using the criteria we have covered in this book.

As you choose your mutual funds, remind yourself that you are an investor, not a collector, so resist the temptation to include all possible candidates in your investment repertoire. You can't afford to shoot in the dark, hoping to hit something. Aim for those that have the proven track record and the lowest levels of risk. You will find it a lot easier to stay on top of your investments if you limit your choices to one or two of the best at any particular time.

Along the Yellow Brick Road

Evaluate your 401(k) investments once a year, just as you would any other mutual fund investment, and make the necessary changes when warranted to make sure that you stay true to your financial objective and risk tolerance. Chapter 9 covers this. Use the same guidelines you have learned in chapter 11 to rebalance your retirement account choices as you approach your retirement goal.

Making sure that you stay on track along the way will pay off when it comes time to break into your retirement piggy bank.

Is That All There Is?

Well, there you have it. You now know how to set up a retirement nest egg so that your golden years will be fulfilling and worry free. You have learned to take slow, methodical steps to make sure that on your road to financial independence, you choose the best possible chauffeur your money can buy to drive you toward your goal. You have taken the time to build a solid foundation. No fads are good enough for your money. You will hear of glitzy funds that may not go the distance, and you will keep on going, knowing well that you can't afford to stray from your established course. Your decisions have been based on track record and proven methods.

The driving force behind your discipline and perseverance is the freedom to enjoy your life to its fullest potential, and you know that it takes money to give you that freedom. After all, you don't want to have to depend on the benevolence of anyone else in your golden years.

Once you have done your homework and opened your retirement account, file your papers away until next year, when it's time to check up on your investments. For now, concentrate on living your life, congratulating yourself for taking the initiative to map your course.

The next and final step in your road to financial freedom is to make sure that you can enjoy your hard-earned nest egg with the confidence that you will never run out of money. A cruise in the Caribbean? Go ahead! Back to school to study literature? Why not? You have planned your life well, and you should enjoy the fruits of your labors however you dang well please!

In the next chapter, I will show you how to spend and enjoy your money shamelessly without the fear of ever running out. After all, you want to make sure that your money lasts at least as long as you do!

CHAPTER THIRTEEN

Enjoying the Fruits of Your Labor

During my childhood in Cuba, I heard a lot of stories. It was part of our family tradition to sit down after dinner and listen to Abuelita tell fables or little morality tales that had scary cautionary morals to them—her not-so-subtle way of trying to teach us children how to behave.

One story that stands out is about a monkey. This monkey was so hungry that he ventured out from his cave into the great unknown to find some food. After hours of searching, he finally came upon a banana tree filled with succulent fruit. The monkey looked around in fear that he would not be the only one spotting such a treasure; he wanted to keep this bounty all to himself. Hurriedly, he proceeded to cut down bunches and bunches of bananas.

On the way back to his cave, the monkey struggled with the thought of what he would do about finding more food once he had finished eating all his bananas. He wished there was a way that he could make his bananas last forever. Lacking a fairy godmonkey to make his wish come true, it occurred to this monkey that he would eat all the banana peels first, saving the best part for last. So that's exactly what this monkey did. One by one, he forced himself to chew and swallow the tart banana skins.

With each bitter swallow, he envisioned the good meal to come. By the time he finished suffering through the agony of eating the yucky skins, he was too full to eat the delicious part that he had so fervently saved for last. Days passed before he could even think of taking another bite. By the time our monkey friend was hungry again, his precious bananas had rotted into an inedible mush.

I have met with hundreds of clients who are saving their "bananas" and eating the peels in the meantime because they are afraid of running out of money. Women especially tend to live below the standard of living that they can well afford because of their fear of not having enough money at some future point in their lives. So they do without the money now. It is sad to see that so many retirees don't enjoy the fruits of their labor while they are still young and healthy. Their lifelong sacrifice ends up being passed on to the next generation, which is not such a terrible thing for those who inherit, but it is sad when there could have been a happy medium between total frugality and wild frivolity.

But this sad scenario doesn't have to be yours. I am happy to tell you that you can have your bananas and eat them, too.

By learning how to invest your money, you are taking the first step to a guilt-free retirement. And by continuing to invest your money while you enjoy the income that it generates, you will increase your chances not only of making your money last but even having some left over to pass on to those you love.

Keeping the Pot Full

Let's pretend that you have a pot filled with money that is intended to cover your housing, clothing, food, entertainment—in fact, all of your necessities and pleasures during your retirement years. You have filled this pot over the years one drop at a time, with the help of the profits you have generated through responsible and disciplined investing.

At retirement time, you are ready to begin withdrawing from this pot that is now growing at a lower but more stable pace than it did during your working years because you switched to an income strategy late in the game to protect your principal.

How much money can you afford to withdraw on a monthly basis? How long will it take for your pot to empty? Is it even truly possible that you could never run out?

In order to answer these questions, you would need to know the following:

1. *How much money you have accumulated.* This will be the total amount of money you have invested (and saved) in all your accounts.

2. *How much money you need to live and enjoy life.* Once you know how much money you now need on a monthly basis, multiply it times twelve to arrive at the yearly amount that you need to receive.

3. *How much money, if any, you are going to receive from any source other than your investments.* This could be from a pension at work, Social Security, etc. If it is a monthly sum, multiply it by twelve.

4. *How much money you need to generate yearly from your account.* Subtract the amount in step 3 from the amount in step 2. The result will be the yearly amount you need to generate from your investments.

5. *The percentage you will be withdrawing annually from your nest egg.* Divide your amount in step 4 by your total amount accumulated (step 1). Multiply the result by 100.

6. *The actual average net return on your investments.* Remember how we determined this return? We went

through the steps to figure this out when we did our yearly checkup on our investments by looking at our ending balance, subtracting it from our deposits, and finding out what percentage we were actually getting on our investments. Make sure you include all your accounts.

Before we go on to figure out how long your money will last, perhaps you want to put your answers into a little chart like this Six Steps for Making a Nest Egg Last chart which you can print out at www.JulieStav.com:

Six Steps for Making a Nest Egg Last

Step 1: Total $ accumulated

Step 2: $ needed per month × 12 months

Step 3: Other monthly sources of income (if monthly, amount × 12)

Step 4: Yearly amount your investment needs to generate
**   (step 2 − step 3)**

Step 5: Percent yearly income represents (step 4 ÷ step 1 × 100)

Step 6: Actual rate of return on your investments

Step 7: Years nest egg will last

Now you need to figure out how long your nest egg will last, based on your current rate of return. Use the following table, which I lovingly call my "Rubber Table," since it will show you how you can stretch your money to last you as long as you want it to. Don't let all these numbers scare you, just take a deep breath. Now, in the left-hand column, find the percentage of your account you will need each year (your amount for step 5). Run your finger across until you are under the column that represents your actual rate of return (step 6). The number in that box is how many years your nest egg will last at your current rate of return.

THE RUBBER TABLE
Years Your Nest Egg Will Last at Different Withdrawal and Return Rates

What percentage of your account will you need per year?	What is your average annual return on all your investments?							
	4%	5%	6%	7%	8%	9%	10%	11%
5%	41 yrs.							
6%	28	36 yrs.						
7%	21	25	33 yrs.					
8%	17	20	23	30 yrs.				
9%	15	16	18	22	28 yrs.			
10%	13	14	15	17	20	26 yrs.		
11%	11	12	13	15	16	19	24 yrs.	
12%	10	11	12	13	14	16	18	23 yrs.

Now let's go through this process together. Let's assume that you have managed to accumulate $400,000 in all of your accounts. This amount includes your 401(k), your IRAs, your savings, your T-bills, and even the money you have stashed in the coffee can at the top of your kitchen cabinet.

Step 1: Total $ accumulated $400,000

Step 2: $ needed per month × 12 months

Step 3: Other sources of income (if monthly, × 12)

Step 4: Yearly amount your investment needs to generate (step 2 − step 3)

Step 5: Percent yearly income represents (step 4 ÷ step 1 × 100)

Step 6: Actual rate of return on your investments

Step 7: Years nest egg will last

You feel that you will need $4,000 per month in order to live the kind of life you worked very hard to achieve. That's $48,000 a year. But wait! You are already getting $1,000 per month from Social Security. This is how you calculate the amount you need on a yearly basis from your investments:

$$\$4,000 - \$1,000 \text{ from SS} = \$3,000 \text{ per month}$$

$$\$3,000 \times 12 \text{ months} = \$36,000 \text{ a year}$$

You will need to withdraw $36,000 from your investments every year in order to be able to enjoy yourself and not worry about money.

Step 1: Total $ accumulated $400,000

Step 2: $ needed per month × 12 months $48,000

Step 3: Other sources of income ($1,000 × 12) = $12,000

Step 4: Yearly amount your investment needs to generate
($48,000−12,000) = $36,000

Step 5: Percent yearly income represents (step 4 ÷ step 1 × 100)

Step 6: Actual rate of return on your investments

Step 7: Years nest egg will last

Now you need to find out the percentage that $36,000 represents of your $400,000. For that, you will divide $36,000 by $400,000 and multiply the result times 100 like this to get a percentage:

$$\$36,000 \div \$400,000 = 0.09$$

$$0.09 \times 100 = 9\%$$

Step 1: Total $ accumulated $400,000

Step 2: $ needed per month × 12 months $48,000

Step 3: Other sources of income ($1,000 × 12) = $12,000

Step 4: Yearly amount your investment needs to generate
($48,000 – $12,000) = $36,000

Step 5: Percent yearly income represents ($36,000 ÷ $400,000 × 100) = 9%

Step 6: Actual rate of return on your investments

Step 7: Years nest egg will last

You will need to withdraw 9 percent of your account each year. But how will that withdrawal affect your remaining balance as the years go by? Let's pretend that your average annual return on all your investments is 8 percent.

Now take a look at The Rubber Table and find 9 percent along the left-hand column. Put your finger there. Find 8 percent across the top, and run your finger until you find the box that corresponds to both of these numbers. The result is twenty-eight years. Your accounts will last you twenty-eight years if you continue to withdraw 9 percent every year while earning an 8 percent average return.

Step 1: Total $ accumulated $400,000

Step 2: $ needed per month × 12 months $48,000

Step 3: Other sources of income ($1,000 × 12) $12,000

Step 4: Yearly amount your investment needs to generate
($48,000 – $12,000) = $36,000

Step 5: Percent yearly income represents ($36,000 ÷ $400,000 × 100) = 9%

Step 6: Actual rate of return on your investments   8%

Step 7: Years nest egg will last   28

There are two ways you could make your money last longer. One is by taking out less from your accounts on a regular basis. That means spending less. Yikes! And the other is by managing to increase your average return by just 1 percent, in which case your money will last forever, since you wouldn't have to touch your principal at all, and your profits would be enough to satisfy your needs. This latter choice is a better idea.

You might accomplish this simply by transferring a little more money from a lower-producing fund to a higher-paying one. For example, you might want to take some money from your bond fund and transfer it to your domestic hybrid fund if the total return of this one is higher. This fine-tuning may be all it takes. Your goal is to generate enough money from your investment accounts to never run out.

As you reevaluate your investments every year, if you are already retired or you depend on your investments for a steady stream of income, it pays to go the extra step and calculate the rate at which you are depleting your account. We can expect to live well into our eighties or nineties, and that means that our money has to last at least as long as we do. You will enjoy spending a lot more if you know that you won't run the risk of running out of money.

Well, there you have it. That's all there is. Use this book. Learn my system with the target, The Five Rs plus Bonus, and the scorecards. Apply it to your investment decisions. Once you do this, you'll never have to spend precious time worrying about your future. Your tomorrows will be funded so your dreams can fill your precious time instead.

Well, we've made it! I am very proud of you for not giving up along the way.

Taking your financial destiny into your own hands is like cleaning out your closet. You may manage to put it off for a good long while, but the time comes when you find yourself wearing the same stuff all the time because you don't even know what you have in there anymore.

You may be "wearing the same stuff" with your money, too, thinking you are in worse shape than you actually are. As scary and uninviting as it may seem at first glance (and second glance, too, come to think of it), once you get immersed in bringing order into your financial life, it will empower you and make you feel that you are in control of your destiny. And that's the greatest feeling you could possibly have.

You may not be able to turn your financial life around in one day, one week, or even one year, but actually planning to make your dreams work out instead of just fantasizing about winning the lottery is more than half the battle.

In getting this far, you have learned about a system with various tools that you can use to choose those investments that will take you to your financial summit. You may choose to use some, part, or all of the guidelines we have reviewed together as a starting point, or you may choose to blaze your own trail. After all, my way is not the only way. In any case, I am honored to have served as a stepping-stone on your journey.

You Are the Star

Before we say so long for now, I would like to share a short story that I heard many years ago when I was teaching first grade in Los Angeles. Its author is unknown, but its lesson serves as a constant reminder of my personal responsibility on this planet. It goes like this:

One day, a man was walking along the seashore. He noticed that during the night, many seashells and starfish had washed up on the shore. Thoroughly enjoying the morning sun and cool sea air, the man strolled for miles along the sand.

Far off in the distance, he saw a small figure dancing. The man felt a sudden joy in witnessing someone celebrating life in such a grand and uninhibited manner. As he drew closer, however, it became apparent that perhaps the figure was not dancing but was repeatedly performing some ritual.

Approaching the small figure, the man noticed that it was a child. The girl was methodically picking up starfish from the shore and tossing them back into the ocean. The man paused for a moment, puzzled, then asked, "Why are you throwing those starfish?"

"If I leave these starfish on the beach," she replied, "the sun will dry them out, and they will die. So I'm throwing them back into the water because I want them to live."

The man was silent for a moment, impressed with the child's thoughtfulness. Then he motioned up and down the miles and miles of beach and said, "But there must be millions of starfish along here! How can you possibly expect to make a difference?"

The young girl pondered the man's words for a moment. Then she slowly leaned over, reached down, and carefully picked up another starfish from the sand. Pulling back, she gently tossed it in the water.

She turned to the man and smiled. "You may be right," she said, "but I made a difference to that one!"

I strongly believe that when the student is ready to learn, the teacher appears, and I hope that I have empowered even one of you to take charge of your financial life. If I have, then my efforts have paid off.

This is just the beginning of your wonderful journey. I encourage you to strive for riches by learning how to nurture what you have already earned. This applies to your personal life as well as your financial life. We are all entitled to enjoy the abundance of the universe, and money is only part of this abundance.

Come visit me on my web site at www.JulieStav.com and share your personal experiences with me. As always, I will welcome your input and would love to hear how my system worked for you in helping you fund your future.

Julie Stav, a financial planner and broker, was born in Cuba and came to the United States as a teenager. A former teacher, she is the founder/owner of Retirement Benefit Systems, a financial planning firm in California, and also runs a network of investment clubs whose members now number in the tens of thousands. Known for her speaking engagements and investment guide videotapes, she has been profiled in the *Los Angeles Times* and other papers, has appeared on Lifetime's *New Attitudes* and *ABC Eyewitness News*, and has appeared numerous times on ABC's *The View*. She is also the author of *Get Your Share*. *Get Your Share* and *Fund Your Future* have been developed into television series on personal finance, which are currently airing on PBS, as is her newest show, *The ABCs of Finance . . . with Julie Stav*.

Visit Julie Stav's web site at www.JulieStav.com